ALL
BATTLE STATIONS
MANNED

ALL
BATTLE STATIONS
MANNED

✳✳

The U.S. Navy in World War II

By JAMES POLING

A THISTLE BOOK

GROSSET & DUNLAP, INC.
a National General Company
Publishers   New York

PHOTO CREDITS
Photo page 190 courtesy of U.S. Coast Guard
All other photographs are courtesy of the
U. S. Navy Department

Library of Congress Catalog Card Number: 72–127730
ISBN 0–448–21396–6 (trade ed.)
ISBN 0–448–26167–7 (library ed.)

For Those Who Fought
and Died

Foreword

In attempting to tell the story of the U.S. Navy in World War II in a short book, only a few gallant men can be mentioned, only a few heroic exploits noted. This is unfortunate, because throughout the war bravery was so commonplace that for every heroic act mentioned in this book a thousand equally courageous deeds could easily have been substituted. For brevity's sake, too, I have had to focus on only the most important campaigns and naval battles of the war. This is again regrettable, since the many minor actions and smaller operations were, of course, necessary to the overall conduct of the war. But to do justice to them all would fill 15 volumes.

That at least is the number of volumes Rear Adm. Samuel Eliot Morison, USNR, filled in writing his monumental *History of the United States Naval Operations in World War Two.* And as I am sure every lesser naval historian has done, I, too, have leaned heavily on Admiral Morison's work; sometimes, I confess, to my discomfort. For it was a humbling experience to discover that someone else knew considerably more than I did about those campaigns of the naval war in the Pacific on which I considered myself something of an authority, because I had taken part in them. On the other hand, I did get some small satisfaction out of finding in my personal notes a few details that apparently were unknown to any of the many naval historians I consulted.

Remsenburg, N.Y.   1970

Contents

CHAPTER 1

✢✢✢✢✢✢✢✢✢✢✢✢✢

"Asleep in the Morning Mist"

The first hint of what lay ahead came at two minutes to four on Sunday morning, 7 December 1941, when the officer of the deck of the destroyer U.S.S. *Ward* awakened his commanding officer, Lt. William W. Outerbridge, to report a disturbing message just received from the minesweeper *Condor*. *Condor* had spotted a suspicious object resembling a submarine periscope in its sweep area, "on westerly course, speed 9 knots." *Condor* and *Ward* were patrolling the sea-lanes leading into Pearl Harbor, the U.S. Pacific Fleet's main base, at Oahu Island, Hawaii. Since the ships' search area was one from which all U.S. submarines were banned, any sub sighted had to be regarded as an enemy vessel.

It wouldn't be an enemy vessel in the formal sense of the word, of course, because Japan and the United States were not yet at war. But on 27 November the U.S. high command in Washington had sent Hawaii a "war warning" message. Addressed to the Army general commanding the islands' land forces and to Adm. Husband E. Kimmel, commander in chief Pacific Fleet, the dispatch ordered them to "execute an appropriate defensive deployment" in anticipation of "an aggressive move by Japan within the next few days . . . against either the Philippines, Thailand, or possibly Borneo."

In view of the world situation the message wasn't wholly unexpected. Most of Europe, including the Netherlands and France, was then in the hands of a German Army that seemed invincible in the first years of World War II. It seemed, too, that Germany might even starve England into surrender with a ruthless submarine blockade. Indeed, Germany was so determined to bring England to her knees that in attacks on neutral U.S. convoys carrying desperately needed goods to the beleaguered British, Nazi U-boats had already sunk seven of our merchant ships and a destroyer and had damaged badly a second destroyer. To counter this violation of our neutrality, we had shifted, fortunately, as it would turn out, from Pearl Harbor to the Atlantic Fleet the aircraft carrier *Yorktown,* three battleships, four cruisers, and two destroyer squadrons. Partly the transfer was made to give our merchant fleet added protection. But to a larger degree it was made in preparation for a war with Germany that appeared inevitable.

We knew that a German war would lead to war with Japan, because in 1940 Japan had signed a Three-Power Pact with Nazi Germany and Fascist Italy, stipulating that if any one of the three went to war with the United States, the other two would join in. But we also knew that Japan herself might draw us into the war without waiting for Germany to force our hand. For events in Europe had given Japan a unique opportunity to steal the helpless Asiatic colonies of the defeated Dutch and French and the besieged English, with their immense supplies of rubber, oil, tin, and other raw materials that the Japanese war machine had to have to carry out a long-cherished ambition—the conquest of all East Asia. And with only the U.S. Pacific Fleet left to oppose them, we fully expected that Japan's warlords would sooner or later take advantage of this once-in-a-lifetime opportunity.

Understandably, then, the war warning came as no great surprise to Admiral Kimmel. But, unfortunately, the dispatch was so misleading it defeated its purpose. For although our intelligence network had learned of Japanese troopship movements in the South China Sea, it had failed to detect Adm. Chuichi Nagumo's Pearl Harbor Striking Force. And his powerful fleet

—two battleships, two heavy cruisers, six aircraft carriers bearing 423 combat planes and a screen of 11 destroyers—had sortied into the North Pacific, Hawaii bound, a full 24 hours before the war warning was dispatched.

Uninformed of Nagumo's move, Admiral Kimmel took the warning at its face value. And since it spoke only of a Japanese attack in waters lying thousands of miles to the west of Hawaii, he executed his defensive deployment accordingly.

West of Hawaii three U.S. island outposts—Wake, Midway, and Guam—stood sentry duty between Japan and Pearl Harbor. Kimmel sent out the aircraft carrier *Enterprise* with an escort of three cruisers and nine destroyers to reinforce Wake with additional Marine fighter planes. The carrier *Lexington,* with three cruisers and five destroyers, was sent to Midway to add 25 scout bombers to the patrol plane strength there. But Kimmel was unable to reinforce our westernmost outpost, Guam, because his only other carrier, *Saratoga,* was en route to San Diego for overhaul.

As for Pearl Harbor, the admiral ordered PBY patrol seaplanes to fly search missions out of Oahu. Unfortunately he concentrated their flights over the sea lanes—all of them southerly—leading to the mouth of the harbor with only an occasional long-range reconnaissance flight to the west and the north. And when he sent minesweepers and destroyers out on patrol, he confined them to the same southerly lanes.

It turned out to be an inexcusably inadequate patrol. Yet it merely reflected an equally inexcusable delusion then held by most navy men—from the Chief of Naval Operations to the lowliest seaman—namely, that Japan would never dare attack Pearl Harbor, knowing it was our most powerful naval base in the Pacific. Thus Kimmel's negligence was born of the Navy's smug belief that Oahu was invulnerable. But he was at least alert enough to order his patrol craft to "shoot on sight" any unauthorized vessels they encountered in their sweeps, war or no war.

With this order in mind, Lieutenant Outerbridge called *Ward* to general quarters the moment he learned of *Condor's* submarine contact. At the first harsh clang of the GQ gong, men still half asleep fumbled into their clothes, sprinting for their battle stations with untied shoelaces and unbuttoned shirts flying. Gun crews rushed topside to their guns. Ammunition handlers hurried below to storage magazines and shell hoists. Damage-control parties ran to their posts, ready to man fire hoses, plug ruptured fuel or steam lines, or patch the ship's hull if it was holed. Medical corpsmen broke out and distributed first-aid equipment. Hatches and scuttles were bolted shut and watertight doors dogged down, to confine fires or flooding to the smallest possible area. Then, as suddenly as it began, the frenzied activity subsided. In less than three minutes every sailor had reached his battle station and now stood quietly awaiting orders.

Calling for all the speed the *Ward's* boilers could provide, Outerbridge conned his ship in the direction *Condor* had given and searched unsuccessfully for nearly an hour. Then he called *Condor* by TBS, the talk-between-ships voice radio circuit. But *Condor* couldn't help him. Her lookouts had lost sight of the periscope—if they'd really seen one—soon after sighting it.

Outerbridge's first impulse was to report a "possible" sub contact to fleet headquarters. Then in view of *Condor's* uncertainty about the sighting, he decided not to. As he said later, there had been so many recent false submarine contacts reported in the vicinity of Oahu that he didn't want to be responsible for crying "Wolf!" once again. Judging from what happened later, it probably wouldn't have made any difference if he had reported the incident.

Having made his decision, Outerbridge gave the order to secure from general quarters. The ship relaxed. The 4-to-8 a.m. watch was set. A new officer of the deck (OOD in navy shorthand) took over the bridge. Sailors not on watch returned to their sleeping quarters. And as captains do under emergency conditions, Outerbridge went to his sea cabin near the bridge, instead of his more comfortable quarters below deck. He didn't get much of a nap, though, because at 6:37 he was again awakened by his OOD. A PBY had sighted a submarine, dropped smoke pots to mark the spot, and relayed the information to the *Ward*.

Back on the bridge, Outerbridge saw off *Ward*'s port bow a periscope and a small conning tower unlike any he'd ever seen. Although he had no way of knowing, it was a midget Japanese submarine that was trying to work its way into Pearl Harbor to coordinate its attack with that of the air armada Nagumo had already launched from his carriers, cruising undetected 275 miles *north* of Oahu's southerly sea approaches. But Outerbridge did know that it was an unauthorized vessel operating in a restricted area. And having his orders, he wasted no time in carrying them out.

After again sounding general quarters and signaling the engine room to come to full speed, he ordered the helmsman to come hard left and head for the sub. As *Ward* gathered speed, the usual GQ reports began coming in over the ship's intercom battle circuit: "Number 2 gun manned and ready, sir . . . Damage control stations manned and ready. . . . Engine room manned . . . Number 1 gun . . . Number 3 gun . . ." When the OOD finally reported, "All battle stations manned and ready, sir," Outerbridge said quietly, "Load all guns. Prepare to drop depth charges. Stand by to commence firing."

He waited until *Ward* had closed to within a hundred yards of the sub, then ordered, "Commence firing." The first shell missed by inches. The second scored a direct hit at the base of the conning tower. And as *Ward*'s stern passed over the diving sub's bow, four depth charges completed the kill.

The time was 6:51 a.m., exactly 64 minutes before the first Japanese bomb hit Pearl Harbor. Thus the opening shots of the war in the Pacific were not fired by the enemy, as is generally

believed, but by the U.S.S. *Ward,* a decrepit old World War I
destroyer that had been officially listed as "overage" in 1934.

At 6:52 Outerbridge radioed, "Have attacked, fired upon,
and dropped depth charges on submarine operating in defensive
area." To emphasize that this was no "wolf" cry, at 6:53 he
repeated the message. To make triply sure that he'd been heard,
he then queried the Oahu naval radio station. The reply was,
"Received and understood."

Received-but-not-believed would have been nearer the truth.
Because when the radio station finally sent the message to fleet
headquarters—after an unexplained delay of 21 minutes—it was
relayed on to three of the fleet's high-ranking officers. As such,
they knew that fleet doctrine called for a general alert in the
event of "a single submarine attack" in the vicinity of Oahu, because this might indicate the presence nearby of an enemy surface
force of fast ships and carriers. Yet knowing this, they still asked
Ward for "further confirmation" of the truth of its report. Then
as the three officers wasted more precious time awaiting *Ward's*
reply—which never came because *Ward* never got the dispatch—
they discussed, as one of them later testified, "what other action
should be taken." In the midst of their discussion, bombs began
exploding.

Thus, through a combination of slow communications and poor
judgment, the Navy lost a priceless opportunity. For when Outerbridge sent his 6:53 message, Nagumo's first wave of planes—
40 torpedo bombers, 51 dive bombers, 51 fighters, and 49 high-
level bombers—was still almost an hour's flying time distant from
Pearl Harbor.

If Outerbridge's dispatch had been acted upon promptly,
American fighter planes could have taken off to intercept the
oncoming Japanese. Every ship in the harbor could have gone
to general quarters, and with their antiaircraft guns manned,
many Jap planes could have been splashed before they released
their deadly missiles. Some ships, too, could have gotten under

way and sailed zigzag courses that would have made them much more difficult targets to hit. Above all else, though, had an alert been sounded at any time prior to 7:40 that morning, many hundreds of lives could have been saved.

It could and should have happened. Instead, as a Jap fighter pilot later wrote, when the attackers reached their goal, "Pearl Harbor was asleep in the morning mist . . . [with] the important ships of the Pacific Fleet strung out at anchor, some side by side."

There were 94 ships in the harbor—70 of them combat ships, the others auxiliary vessels such as tankers and supply ships. Aside from the few men on watch, most of the ships' crews were below deck, lazily dressing to face the usual quiet routine of a sabbath morning. On the fighting ships, only about one in four antiaircraft guns was manned by the watch. And in keeping with peacetime custom, all ready ammunition was in locked boxes whose keys were held by each ship's OOD. Ironically, too, of all the ships present only those the Japanese considered "important"— the great battleships—were grouped together. They formed an ideal target, a bull's-eye so large it was hard to miss.

When the first attack wave sighted Oahu at about 7:40, most of the fighters and dive bombers left the formation to demolish the island's five military airfields. With the fields' antiaircraft guns neither manned nor supplied with ready ammunition, the attackers met only token opposition. It came from a few courageous men—some still in pajamas or underwear—who braved strafing bullets to wrench machine guns off parked planes and blaze away. Others fought back with rifles and pistols. Some even hurled hammers and wrenches at Jap planes swooping low over the runways—probably to the amusement of the grinning Japs who, bombing and strafing at hangar-top level, quickly knocked out of action 363 of the 500 planes on the ground that morning.

While the threat of air opposition was being eliminated, the

The U.S. destroyer Shaw *blows up during Japanese attack on Pearl Harbor, December 7, 1941.*

torpedo planes and high-level bombers headed for Battleship Row, the raid's main target. Battleship Row ran along the easterly shore of low-lying Ford Island in the center of the harbor. Its moorings were massive concrete quays set in a straight line a short distance off the island shore. The battleship *Nevada* occupied the most northerly berth. Behind her came *Arizona,* followed by *Tennessee* and *West Virginia,* moored side by side. Then came another pair, *Maryland* and *Oklahoma,* also moored in tandem. At the end of the row was *California,* alone in the southernmost berth. Another battleship, *Pennsylvania,* was across the harbor in dry dock. (*Colorado,* the Pacific Fleet's ninth dreadnought, was back in the States being overhauled.)

Flying undetected above a dense cloud cover hanging at about 6,000 feet, the strike commander, Capt. Mitsuo Fuchida, brought his planes over the target at 7:50. He dove once through the clouds to check his bearings, then gave the order to attack. His specially trained pilots, aware of the American practice of mooring battleships in pairs, knew exactly what to do. The 40 torpedo planes immediately dove to the low altitudes required for launching torpedoes—40 to 80 feet above the water—then leveled off and headed for the five battleships with exposed hulls. The 49 bombers, specially armed with converted 16-inch armor-piercing shells designed to penetrate steel decks and explode in a ship's bowels, followed in a shallow glide. Their main mission was to cripple the two battleships whose hulls could not be reached by torpedoes; *Maryland,* lying inboard of *Oklahoma,* and *Tennessee,* protected by *West Virginia.*

The attack came so suddenly that its momentarily stunned victims never knew for sure which ship was hit first. But by 7:58, three minutes after the poorly aimed first bomb exploded on a Ford Island seaplane ramp, at least two battleships were already doomed and hundreds of American seamen dead.

Oklahoma was probably the first casualty. At least, she was the only ship in the row that never had a chance to fight back, because her crew was still running to battle stations when three torpedoes tore her hull open. With no watertight doors dogged down and no time to counterflood, the sea poured in so fast that it was obvious that she was due to capsize any minute. So the "abandon ship" order was given—just as two more torpedoes struck. Now fatally stricken, *Oklahoma* began to roll over "as slowly and stately as if she were tired and wanted to rest," according to one observer. And she didn't stop rolling until her mast jammed in the mud, leaving her bottom up. It was all over in 8 minutes.

Oklahoma lost 415 men out of a crew of 1,354. Many of her survivors climbed aboard *Maryland,* tied alongside, to offer their help. But *Maryland* needed no help. Protected from torpedoes by *Oklahoma,* she got off with only two bomb hits and minor casualties, and was the first of the battle fleet to return to active service.

Berthed alone and horribly mangled by torpedoes in the first minutes of the attack, *Arizona* got her death blow just as *Oklahoma* turned turtle. It came from a bomb that crashed through *Arizona*'s forecastle and set off her forward magazines. Like an erupting volcano, her exploding ammunition threw shattered steel, flame, and smoke 500 feet into the air, and with one searing flash wiped out most of the men topside, including a rear admiral who was last seen manning an antiaircraft gun. The torn and gutted battlewagon then sank so fast that hundreds more of her crew were trapped below deck.

Tragically, *Arizona*'s casualties were more than half the toll the entire fleet suffered at Pearl Harbor—1,103 men killed out of 1,400 aboard. Her skeleton and most of theirs are still there today. In their honor, the U.S.S. *Arizona* has been kept on the Navy's roster of active ships, with a color guard for a crew. And every day her crew raises and lowers her ensign on a mast rising from a monument built over the *Arizona*'s remains.

Moored together ahead of *Arizona* were *Tennessee* and *West*

Virginia. As the inboard ship, *Tennessee* took damaging bomb hits on two of her turrets. But she suffered even greater damage from fires started by flaming debris raining down on her decks from *Arizona.* To add to her plight, blazing fuel oil from *Arizona*'s ruptured tanks drifted down on her. *Tennessee* tried to drive the flaming oil away by churning the water with her propellers. But it didn't work, and for hours the burning fuel kept her hull and decks hot enough to burn flesh. Even so, her half-roasted damage-control parties finally brought her fires under control. Meanwhile, her gun crews shot down five Jap bombers.

Alongside *Tennessee, West Virginia* took six torpedoes and two bombs and, like *Oklahoma,* would have capsized with a tremendous loss of life but for the alertness of two young officers. One was her OOD, an ensign who ordered, "Away all fire and rescue parties" the moment he saw the first bomb hit the seaplane ramp. By bringing everyone topside on the double, his order saved countless lives. But the ship remained in grave danger, because the weight of the water pouring through the torpedo holes was causing her to list so sharply that her guns had to be served by a double row of ammunition handlers—one to pass the ammunition, the other to hold the passers upright. As the list worsened, a youthful lieutenant finally took it upon himself to order the port compartments counterflooded. This corrected the list enough to prevent capsizing, and the ship finally settled to the bottom with only a 15-degree tilt.

Had the lieutenant waited for a counterflooding order from his commanding officer, it would never have come. For *West Virginia*'s skipper, Captain Bennion, lay dying on the bridge, his abdomen torn open by bomb fragments. However, he remained conscious long enough to give one final command. When flames began to engulf the bridge, he ordered two junior officers to abandon their attempt to save him and jump to safety before they too were trapped. Captain Bennion was one of the 105 men killed on *West Virginia* out of a crew of about 1,500.

Moored alone at the southern end of Battleship Row, *California* was in the poorest condition to take a hit, because she was preparing for an admiral's inspection. Knowing how admirals pry, her crew had not only opened all her scuttles, hatches, and watertight doors, but also removed the manhole covers leading to her double bottom. Thus, when two torpedoes ripped her hull open, there was nothing to stop the sea from surging through the entire "unbuttoned" ship. And as the water rose, *California* too settled onto the mud, leaving her main deck awash and only her superstructure showing.

Alone at the northern end of the row, *Nevada* got her guns into action in time to splash two and turn away the rest of the torpedo planes that attacked her, but not before one dropped a "fish" that tore a 45- by 30-foot hole in her side. Prompt counterflooding, however, quickly brought her back to even keel. Moreover, her power plant was still working and she had steam up on two boilers. So her temporary commanding officer, a reserve lieutenant commander standing by for seven higher-ranking officers who were on weekend leave, decided to get the ship under way. And once he did, he handled *Nevada* like a veteran as he headed her down channel toward the open sea.

It seemed for a time, too, that the battleship might get clear, because at 8:25 the first wave of Jap planes broke off their attack. At 8:40, though, Nagumo's follow-up strike of 170 planes arrived to finish whatever the first wave had left undone. This second strike quickly brought *Nevada* to a halt. For amidst geysers of water from a dozen near-misses she took three direct bomb hits, including one that "opened the forecastle like a sardine can." Now flooding fast, *Nevada,* too, was in danger of sinking. What was worse, if she sank in mid-channel, she would block the mouth of Pearl Harbor to all but the smallest craft. Hurriedly, two tugs were sent to her side. Bravely fighting their way through the flames fanning out from her thoroughly demolished topside, the tugs nosed the battlewagon out of the channel into shallow water, where she settled harmlessly on hard sand.

While *Nevada* was being worked over, other second-wave Jap planes hunted down whatever targets they could find. Many bombers went for *Pennsylvania,* out of torpedo reach in dry dock. In reply, she threw up such heavy antiaircraft fire that she took but one bomb hit and lost only 18 men. But several bombs meant for her plunged into destroyers *Cassin* and *Downes,* in the same dry dock, and left them smoldering wrecks. Other bombers sank a minelayer, a repair ship, a floating dry dock, a target ship and reduced a third destroyer to junk. Still others crippled three light cruisers, including *Raleigh,* whose captain's battle garb consisted of nothing but a pair of blue pajamas.

At 9:45 the Jap planes, all bombs and torpedoes spent, headed back to their carriers. The battle was over.

Thus in less than two hours the Japanese accomplished their mission—wrecking what to their minds was the one great obstacle to their dream of conquest, the Battle Line of the Pacific Fleet.

They left behind an appalling stricken Pearl Harbor. Eighteen warships—including seven of the eight great battlewagons—were either sunk or damaged. Well over half of Oahu's aircraft were out of action. And the casualties were frightful—2,403 Americans killed or missing, another 1,178 wounded. In this one battle the Navy alone lost about three times as many men as it lost in World War I and the Spanish-American War combined.

And all of this carnage had been wrought at the triflng cost to the Japanese of 29 planes and their pilots.

Yet it might have been worse. For one thing, Admiral Nagumo would live to regret the fact that he hadn't caught the fleet's three carriers—*Enterprise, Saratoga,* and *Lexington*—at anchor in the harbor. For another, his pilots overlooked two prime targets. They didn't bomb the fuel-oil tank farm that was filled to capacity. Had the fleet lost its fuel supply, it would have been months before it could even put to sea, much less counterattack. The Japs also ignored the ship-repair shops. And left intact, these shops did an astonishingly quick job on the damaged vessels. True, *Oklahoma* and *Arizona* were beyond salvage. And it took months to refloat and repair *California, Nevada,* and *West Virginia.* But almost unbelievably, within seven weeks *Pennsylvania, Tennessee,* and *Maryland* were back at sea, along with the three damaged cruisers. Even so, the fleet had been dealt such a staggering blow that the balance of naval power in the Pacific was for the time being decisively tipped toward the Rising Sun of Japan.

In Washington, D.C., the next day, a grim-faced and angry President Franklin D. Roosevelt addressed Congress. He began, "Yesterday, December 7, 1941—a date which will live in infamy —the United States of America was suddenly and deliberately attacked by naval and air forces of the empire of Japan . . ."

The raid on Pearl Harbor, he made clear, was not an isolated episode. There had been other raids, equally treacherous and equally well-planned—so many in fact that it was obvious that for months Japan had been secretly plotting and preparing to conquer East Asia and most of the island territories of the Pacific by brute force. The President then named some of the places other than Pearl Harbor that had been attacked without warning in the previous 24 hours:

Yesterday the Japanese government also launched an attack against Malaya.
Last night Japanese forces attacked Hong Kong.
Last night Japanese forces attacked Guam.
Last night Japanese forces attacked the Philippine Islands.
Last night the Japanese attacked Wake Island.
And this morning the Japanese attacked Midway Island.
. . . Hostilities exist . . . our people, our territory, and our interests are in grave danger . . . I ask that the Congress declare that, since the unprovoked and dastardly attack by

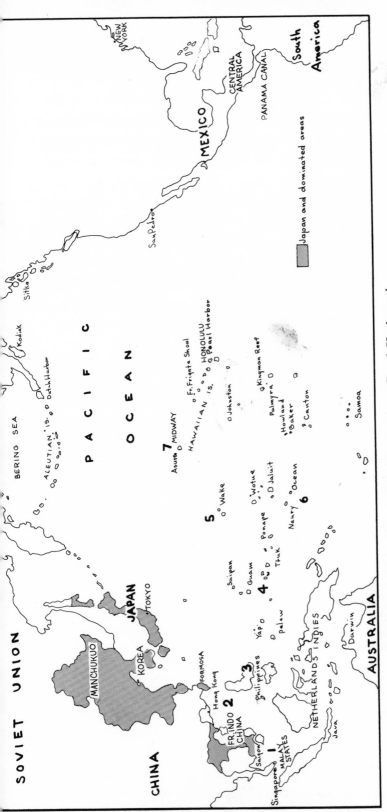

In the 24 hours that followed their air attack on Pearl Harbor, the Japanese struck at (1) British Malaya (2) Hong Kong (3) the Philippines (4) Guam (5) Wake Island (6) Nauru and Ocean Islands and (7) Midway Island.

Japan on Sunday, December 7, 1941, a state of war has existed between the United States and the Japanese Empire.

Congress so declared. And three days later Nazi Germany and Fascist Italy lived up to the Three-Power Pact by declaring war on the United States.

Thus we became belligerents in the greatest of all wars. It was already two years old and would last another four. It menaced three-quarters of the earth's population. The armed forces on both sides totaled more than 100 million. Eleven million of them died, including half a million Americans. There were tens of millions of civilian casualties. The war cost an estimated $1 quadrillion—a figure beyond all comprehension. Even more incomprehensible, and infinitely more appalling, was the war's immeasurable cost in human suffering.

CHAPTER 2

✲✲✲✲✲✲✲✲✲✲✲✲

Prelude to Battle

Most of the root causes of World War II can be traced back to World War I, ironically proclaimed in its day as "the war to end all war." Indeed, the peace treaty forced on Germany by the victorious Allies—England, France, Italy, and the United States —was so vengeful and so politically unrealistic that it almost guaranteed another war.

For one thing, the treaty tore apart old nations and formed new ones with an eye more to weakening Germany than to the wishes of many of the people it abruptly thrust behind new boundaries. As an example, in the creation of Czechoslovakia the Allies included within its borders the Sudetenland—and a large percentage of Sudetenlanders were Germans whose only loyalty was to their Fatherland. In giving Poland nationhood the Allies set up a "Polish Corridor" that not only separated East Prussia from the rest of Germany but included the almost wholly German city of Danzig.

Even more unrealistically, the Saar Valley was taken from Germany with the understanding that its coal, always the chief source of fuel for German industry, would for 15 years go exclusively to France. Without coal, a postwar industrial recovery in Germany was virtually impossible. Yet the treaty foolishly went on to demand that Germany pay the Allies every cent the conflict had cost them—a demand no one country, much less war-impoverished Germany, could ever meet.

In these and other ways, as we will see, the treaty played directly into the hands of the man who started World War II—Adolf Hitler.

Following the signing of the treaty, a worldwide organization of countries—both large and small—was formed. Called the League of Nations, its members were supposed to work together to ensure peace in the world forevermore. But as events proved, the League's member nations were too weak-kneed to police the world when the need arose. And the League was further weakened when America refused to join it. Instead, the United States turned its back on the outside world and tried to isolate itself from the international scene completely. Because of this, one historian has said that in the 1920's and early thirties, when new war clouds were gathering, "While France and England may have slept, America not only slept but snored."

During those Rip Van Winkle years of American diplomacy, Lenin's Bolsheviks, not content with having gained control of Russia, were trying to overthrow the weak and unsettled governments of Germany and Italy, among others. But most people in those countries, fearing everything communism stood for, were willing to accept in its place any leader or any form of government that promised to protect them from the Red Menace.

This provided an ideal climate for the growth of dictatorships. And the first to profit from it was Benito Mussolini who, with his Fascist Party, took over Italy in the twenties and immediately began rebuilding his country's war machine. He was followed in Germany by Adolf Hitler with his Nazi Party. Of the two, Hitler was the more evil, but both dictators had in common a lust for world power, a contempt for international law, and a ruthless determination to seize any country they could overwhelm, —once they had built up their armies, navies, and air forces. And being expert propagandists, they publicized the growing strength of their armed forces so skillfully that the other nations of the Western World, ourselves included, soon developed a healthy respect for their military might—without, however, building matching forces to offset it.

Hitler became Germany's leader in 1934, and a year later thumbed his nose at the victors of the first war by establishing a military draft. This was a violation of the peace treaty, but he got away with it with no more than a whimper of outrage from the former Allies, which he of course ignored. Then Mussolini invaded and conquered defenseless Ethiopia. And the League of Nations, instead of going to Ethiopia's aid, did nothing more than impose economic sanctions against Italy. It was a mere slap on the wrist. But even so it was enough to anger the arrogant Mussolini and drive him into Hitler's camp.

Having seen neither the League nor any of the so-called Great Powers had the will to fight, Hitler next sent his newly drafted troops in to reoccupy the Saar Valley. This gave him the coal his armament factories needed to produce a stockpile of tanks, planes, and other weapons. And it gave him another easy, bloodless victory over Germany's recent conquerors who let him get away with it.

Then in 1936 Francisco Franco, seeking to become dictator of Spain, plunged his country into a bloody civil war. Hitler and Mussolini rushed to aid Franco. The freedom-loving Spaniards who opposed Franco won Russian support. And soon all three outside countries were testing new weapons and new concepts of military tactics on Spanish soil. France, England, and the United States, on the other hand, stood aloof from the struggle, timidly shutting their eyes to the all-too-obvious fact that the Spanish conflict was a grim dress rehearsal for a new European war.

Early in 1938 it was clear that, with the backing of Hitler and Mussolini, Franco was winning his war. Confident now that he could defy the world with impunity, Hitler then marched his troops into Austria and annexed the country in a bloodless military coup—without hearing so much as a harsh word from the League of Nations. Next, in April 1938, Hitler demanded the return of the Sudetenland to Germany, and for the first time met with token opposition. France and England sent diplomats to Munich to protest to Hitler. He toyed with them, tricked them with false promises and veiled threats, and they, being militarily unprepared for war, quickly backed down. Deserted by her "friends," Czechoslovakia yielded to the threat of invasion and gave up the Sudetenland.

Turning his eyes next to the Polish Corridor, Hitler claimed that Danzig rightfully belonged to the Fatherland because it was a city "thoroughly German in language and tradition." Poland in turn appealed to England. And the British, realizing at last that Hitler's mania for conquest threatened them too, agreed to fight if Germany invaded Poland.

Hitler, whose plans for invading Poland were already laid, had no fear of England. But he wasn't yet prepared for a two-front war. And to make sure he didn't get involved in one he seduced his arch-enemy, Stalin, into signing a nonaggression pact by promising to divide Poland with Russia. Then on 1 September, 1939, Nazi troops stormed into Poland. And on 3 September, England and a now-aroused France both declared war on Germany.

With Poland conquered before England and France could marshal their forces, Hitler was content to hold the British and French at bay until he had his armies regrouped and redeployed. Then in the spring of 1940 he set his divisions in motion again. In April they swallowed up Denmark and invaded Norway. In May they rolled over Holland and Belgium and on into France. There, quickly piling victory on victory, they reached the French channel ports by May 26, overwhelming the French Army and forcing the British to ferry what was left of theirs back home.

On 22 June, the French withdrew from the war and signed an armistice with Germany that handed over three-fifths of France, including its Atlantic and Channel coasts, to German occupation. Left unoccupied was the country's central and Mediterranean regions, an area known as "Vichy France" because it was ruled from the city of Vichy by a puppet French government set up by the Germans. Yet despite the sweeping terms of the armistice, the French Navy, which the Germans wanted, escaped their grasp. Many French warships were scuttled to keep them out of Hitler's hands, while others for the same reason fled to ports in French North Africa.

At this point Hitler was master of Western Europe. Yet England still stood firm. So in August he ordered his famed air force, the *Luftwaffe*, to bomb England into submission. But the vastly outnumbered British Royal Air Force, making up in courage for what it lacked in planes, soundly thrashed the *Luftwaffe*. Then Hitler sent his submarines out to prevent any supplies from reaching Britain, hoping to starve her into capitulation. Since his U-boats could now operate out of French rather than Baltic ports, which extended their range by hundreds of miles and enabled them to roam the entire Atlantic, he was confident his plan would work.

While Hitler was preoccupied with England, Mussolini invaded Egypt. To muddle matters further, he then invaded Greece without even bothering to consult his partner. From the beginning, though, his troops fought poorly in both campaigns. In fact, in December the Italians in Egypt took such a thorough licking from Britain's Desert Army that Hitler, to his great annoyance, had to send an armored division to North Africa to save the Italians' hide. Worse still, the English showed no signs of wavering. And in Greece the Italian Army was clearly stalemated.

Held to a standstill on all fronts, Hitler in his anger and frustration made his great mistake. He decided to invade Russia, defeat her, and then deal with the stubborn British.

Once the decision was made, curiously enough, the tide of war again began to flow in favor of the Axis Powers, as the alliance of Germany and Italy was called. The conquest of Yugoslavia, a necessary preliminary to an attack on Russia, went smoothly. In Greece, a German Army succeeded where Mussolini's had failed. In North Africa, Nazi armor began rolling back the British. And Hitler somehow managed to mass 3 million men on the Russian border without arousing Stalin's suspicions.

In June 1941, Hitler gave the invasion order that treacherously broke his nonaggression pact with Russia, and by November his armies had smashed through to the outskirts of Moscow. At this point, many people took it for granted that Russia would soon have to surrender and leave all of Europe in the merciless hands of Hitler and Mussolini. But a situation beyond the dictators' control was developing, and when it came to a head the entire nature of the war would change. For the long-smoldering enmity between Japan and the United States was about to break into flames. And when it did, Hitler and Mussolini would be among those the flames would eventually consume.

For this they would have in large part only themselves to blame, because they by their own ruthless acts had been the first to stir America from her isolationist slumber. In fact, as early as 1939 President Roosevelt had warned Hitler that Germany's brutal rape of Europe posed a threat to this country's international interests that we could not long ignore.

Most Americans, however, were slower to awaken than the President, and although they sympathized with France and England, they still didn't want to get involved in an overseas war. Yet despite their reluctance, after the fall of France the President nonetheless managed to win congressional support for what he called a short-of-war program. The support was given because France's defeat seemed to open the way to Hitler's acquiring bases in England. If he took over North Africa too, there was a good chance that he would then try to set up Nazi governments in South America and the French, English, and

Dutch West Indies. And this was a threat the United States could not tolerate.

Roosevelt's first short-of-war move in 1940 was to give England 50 old destroyers to help her fight the U-boat campaign, in exchange for U.S. naval and air bases in the British West Indies, Newfoundland, and Bermuda. Next, the Congress approved the President's request for $4 billion to begin building a two-ocean navy. Following this, in March 1941 the Congress passed the Lend-Lease Act to make it lawful for us to supply arms on a buy-now-pay-later basis to any nation fighting the Axis. Our Navy then began convoying ships carrying Lend-Lease goods to a mid-ocean meeting point (MOMP) south of Iceland, where the British Navy then took over. In a move that brought us even nearer to war, the President also sent Marines to Iceland to keep Germany from seizing that country and using it as an air and U-boat base from which convoys in the MOMP area could easily be attacked.

Meanwhile, British and American military strategists had secretly reached an agreement known as the ABC-1 Plan. Under this plan, we promised that, if and when Japan and the United States were drawn into the war, we would exert our primary military effort in the European theater. This Beat the Axis First policy grew out of our belief that Germany had a far greater war potential than Japan. It didn't mean that we intended to sit on our hands while Japan ran rampant in Asia. Rather, it meant that in the Pacific we would limit ourselves to delaying and harassing tactics until, with the defeat of the Axis, we could fall on Japan with our full force.

Japan had to be considered in the ABC-1 Plan because ever since World War I she and the United States had been following such a dangerous collision course that a head-on meeting of the two now seemed almost unavoidable.

In the first world conflict, Japan had waited shrewdly to enlist in the Allied cause until it was too late for her troops to reach

Europe in time to fight, but not too late for them to capture three Pacific island groups owned by Germany—the Marianas, the Carolines, and the Marshalls. As a reward for her so-called "service" to the cause, at the war's end all of the islands, in the three groups, but one were placed under Japanese control. The exception was Guam, in the Marianas, which we had taken from Spain in the Spanish-American War and kept as a naval base when Spain later sold the rest of the Marianas Islands to Germany.

The transfer of the island groups, which Japan quickly fortified, angered American military planners; because it gave the Japanese strategically located naval and air bases, flanking the sea lanes from Pearl Harbor to our westernmost Pacific outposts —Guam and the Philippines. Had we joined the League of Nations we almost certainly could have blocked the transfer. But we didn't and, as we will see, we lived to regret it.

During the 1920's, although the United States and Japan kept a wary eye on each other, their relations neither improved nor worsened. But throughout that decade a Japanese counterpart of Nazism was gathering strength. Called the *Kodo-Ha* movement, its first aim was to bring Japan under military control. Its second goal was to "free" China, India, the Philippines, and other Asian countries from "foreign imperialists" by bringing them all under Japanese rule.

Kodo-Ha first showed its ambitious hand in 1931 when Japan invaded the northern Chinese territory of Manchuria, a region rich in coal and iron. After renaming the territory Manchukuo, Japan then claimed it as its own. America reacted, but only with angry words which of course broke no Japanese bones. China herself, weakly ruled by Chiang Kai-shek, was powerless to do anything more than appeal to the League of Nations. In response, the League ruled that none of its member nations could legally recognize or deal with the puppet state of Manchukuo.

With this, Japan withdrew from the League and contented

herself during the next few years with a consolidation of her foothold on the Chinese mainland. Then in 1937, without bothering to declare war, she invaded China proper. This led to a drawn-out, indecisive war which by 1940 was costing Japan much more than she could afford. And this time, with Roosevelt as President, America hit Japan where it hurt. We froze all Japan's assets in the U.S., which were worth about $100 million, and placed a boycott on all Japanese goods. England and the Netherlands, though in no position to defend their Far Eastern territories, followed suit.

Japan now felt that she was faced with either war or economic ruin. But for the moment she was in a state of indecision. Under Japanese law Emperor Hirohito held absolute rule, yet on matters of foreign policy he usually took his cabinet's advice. And his cabinet was divided. His prime minister, Prince Fumimaro Konoye, wanted a peaceful settlement with the United States. His war minister, Gen. Hideki Tojo, wanted war, in part because he hated America and in part because he was both the head of the *Kodo-Ha* movement and a military dictator at heart.

Prince Konoye tried for a time to persuade the U.S. to end its economic war on Japan. But Roosevelt refused to lift a finger until Japan withdrew from China. Knowing his cabinet would never agree to this, Konoye resigned in October 1941. He was replaced by Tojo who, as prime minister now, became the virtual dictator of Japan.

(Unlike Hitler and Mussolini, Tojo had not publicized but long kept secret the extent to which Japan had been enlarging her armed forces. Thus on the eve of Pearl Harbor, when we thought Japan's Navy was inferior to the Pacific Fleet, the actual combat ship score was: Pacific Fleet 9 battleships, Japan 10; Pacific Fleet 3 carriers, Japan 10; Pacific Fleet 24 cruisers, Japan 35; Pacific Fleet 80 destroyers, Japan 111; Pacific Fleet 55 submarines, Japan 64. Furthermore, Japan's *Yamato* and *Mushshi* were the largest battleships ever built, with 18-inch guns whose 3,200-pound shells were 50 percent heavier than the 16-inch shells of the biggest American naval guns.)

As prime minister, Tojo continued to carry on diplomatic talks with Washington. But he was a fanatic who believed that with the French and Dutch defeated and the English besieged the destined time had come for Japan to throw off the yoke of "foreign imperialism" which had so long thwarted her dream of ruling all Asia. So while he went through what to him were merely the motions of negotiating with Washington, he at the same time secretly stationed his forces in accordance with a master war plan which he had had his staff draw up months before he took over the premiership. In fact, by 1 December 1941— the day he finally persuaded Hirohito that war was inevitable and won the Emperor's sanction to the conflict—Tojo had already set the plan in motion, for Admiral Nagumo's Task Force was even then at sea, Hawaii-bound.

The Japanese master plan was: First, the crippling of the U.S. Pacific Fleet prior to the declaration of war. Second, destruction of the British and American forces on the Malay Peninsula and Luzon in the Philippines. Third, before the British and American navies could recover, a quick seizure of the Philippines, Guam, Wake, Hong Kong, Borneo, British Malaya (including Singapore), and Sumatra. Fourth, then a conquest of the richest prize, Java, and the rest of the Dutch islands. Fifth, a massive effort to siphon out of Malaya and Indonesia the oil, rubber, tin and other raw materials needed to keep the Japanese war machine running in high gear.

To safeguard her conquests, Japan would establish a line of military strongpoints running from her own northernmost Kurile Islands, through Wake, the Marshall Islands, and the Malay Barrier (Sumatra, Bali, Timor, and Java) to the Burmese-India border. With this defensive perimeter, Japan would then hold formidable bases from which her navy and air force could easily cut the lines of communications between Australia and

New Zealand and the Anglo-American powers, which would then be forced to sue for peace. With her Western enemies defeated, Japan would be free to conquer China. Then a third of the world's land mass and more than half of its people would be under the absolute control of the Emperor.

It was the most ambitious and far-reaching plan of conquest in modern history. And it almost worked, since at the outbreak of hostilities our Navy was in an almost impossible position. Because although numerous new warships were under construction, for many long months the Navy would have to fight with just what it had at the moment. And that meant fighting a two-ocean war with an old and smaller than one-ocean fleet. Yet in the end a Pacific Fleet that rose from the ashes of Pearl Harbor would turn Tojo's dream of conquest into a nightmare. And in the Atlantic and Mediterranean a smaller but no less-courageous fleet would play an important part in toppling Mussolini and Hitler.

CHAPTER 3

✚✚✚✚✚✚✚✚✚✚✚✚✚

Silencing the Kettledrum

In the Atlantic, a convoy being escorted to MOMP by U.S. destroyers was intercepted by the Nazi submarine *U-562* on 31 October 1941. Although the United States and Germany were still at peace, when U.S.S. *Reuben James* closed on the sub with her depth charges set for an attack, she was herself torpedoed and sunk with a ghastly toll of life; 115 men out of a crew of about 160. This single prewar episode probably did more to put the American public in a mood to fight Germany than all of Hitler's European atrocities combined.

Comdr. Griffith Coale. who witnessed the sinking from a nearby destroyer, wrote of it:

"A loud explosion . . . Know instantly it is a torpedo, not a depth charge. Reach deck with general quarters still rasping. It is not us. A mile ahead a rising cloud of smoke hangs over the black loom of a ship. With a terrific roar, a column of orange flame towers high in the sky as her magazines go up. All of the ship forward of No. 4 stack disappears. We move rapidly down on her as her stern rises into the air, then slides slowly into the sea. A moment, and two grunting jolts as her exploding depth charges toss men and debris into the air. Suddenly my nostrils are filled with the sickly stench of fuel oil . . .

"We hear cursing, praying, and hoarse shouts for help from her men who are like black shiny seals in the oily waters. We rig cargo nets over the side, make lines ready for heaving. 'We are the *Reuben James'* men!' comes a chorus from one raft, and then we know. The spirit of these huddled greasy forms overloading the life rafts is magnificent. But the bobbing blobs of isolated men are pitiful . . . choking with oil and water, they are like small animals caught in molasses.

"Men are drifting toward us but the hove lines are slipping through their oily hands. Soon many grasp our cargo nets, but our ship's roll breaks their weak and slippery hold. Instantly men go over the side, and in no time several of our crew are making lines fast around the slimy survivors so that strong arms above on the deck can heave them aboard. The first man is hauled over the amidship rail vomiting oil . . .

"It is a desperately hard job to get these men aboard. Our men work feverishly . . . But the horizon is red with dawn, and the increasing light makes us an easy target for the sub which must be lurking nearby. The captain says, 'I can't risk the ship and her company much longer.' Now there are two or three left. Suddenly a submarine contact directly astern! Another destroyer gets it too.

"There is nothing for it . . . we leap away, leaving two survivors to swirl astern. We search, lose the contact, return, and the other destroyer picks up 11 survivors while we circle her. We hope she got the two we had to leave. A third destroyer comes back to relieve us, with orders to search the spot until noon, and we with 36 survivors, and the other rescue ship, catch up with the fleeing convoy at 25 knots."

While the sinking outraged the American public, certain facts in fairness must be faced. For one, our gift of 50 destroyers to the British had outraged the Germans. For another, we had abandoned all pretense of neutrality and firmly allied ourselves with Britain, and later Russia, when we passed the Lend-Lease Act. Moreover, in passing it Congress had knowingly violated international laws which stipulated that it was illegal for a neutral nation to lend money or give credit to a belligerent country or for its merchant ships to trade with such a nation. By law, any supplies we furnished Britain and Russia were supposed to be paid for in cash and transported in their own ships. (To justify our lawbreaking we argued that we were unneutral only toward the two Axis powers, as compared to their violation of the neutrality of a dozen defenseless nations.)

We also openly sided with Britain when we landed Marines in Iceland in July 1941 and freed the 15,000 British troops already garrisoned there to fight in North Africa, where they were desperately needed. And we took sides again when in the same month the U.S. Navy began to escort ships of other nations, not just our own, from American ports to their rendezvous point with the Royal Navy at MOMP.

Since the German Navy understandably regarded these moves as acts of war it's not surprising, then, that in self-defense one of its U-boats sank *Reuben James.* Nor is it surprising that on 17 October the destroyer *Kearney* was also torpedoed—fortunately with the loss of only 11 men—while trying to attack a Nazi sub. All things considered, what is surprising is that the shooting war which began in the Atlantic 8 weeks prior to Germany's formal declaration of war in mid-December was as limited as it was.

Even so, this brief undeclared war gave us a bitter hint of things to come. For in the two engagements only the U-boats drew blood. And this was a clue to our greatest naval weakness. We were totally unprepared for all-out anti-submarine warfare, as Adm. Karl Doenitz, Germany's able U-boat chief, proved with a vengeance in the opening rounds of the Battle of the Atlantic.

As it happens, the Battle of the Atlantic was the longest uninterrupted naval engagement of the war; a running fight with U-boats that went on night and day, with its outcome hanging in the balance for two years. Consequently, following its course will take us far ahead of the story of naval warfare on other fronts. But this is necessary, because so much was at stake in the

Battle of the Atlantic that it has to be seen as a single action if its full significance is to be understood.

Hitler summed up the battle's importance to the Axis when he told his admirals, "There can never be any letup in submarine warfare. The Atlantic is our first line of defense in the West." For the Allies, the battle was all-important because their only hope of conquering Hitler lay in keeping the Atlantic sea-lanes open for supplies, and for ferrying a U.S. Army to England for the eventual invasion of Europe. Yet they came so close to losing the battle that Great Britain's wartime Prime Minister, Winston Churchill, later said, "The only thing that ever really frightened me during the war was the U-boat peril."

He had reason to be frightened, because by the end of 1942 U-boats had sunk so much shipping that England, left with only a scant 3-month supply of food, was beginning "to eat her own tail." Indeed, in 1942 alone German torpedoes found so many targets that they forced the U.S. to cut back on the production of badly needed combat ships and concentrate instead on building cargo vessels. In addition, Roosevelt also had to slow down our troop-training program. It was pointless to train more troops than could be transported overseas in the ships we had left at the year's end.

Yet in the first month of the war Allied shipping losses fell off sharply. We soon learned why. Admiral Doenitz spent the month redeploying his U-boats. Knowing we had to use the Atlantic Fleet to protect transatlantic convoys, he had withdrawn 20 of his ace U-boat commanders from European waters and sent them to the American east coast, where he rightly guessed that single nonconvoyed merchantmen could be knocked down like tenpins. Thus in the early days of January 1942 a file of 20 submarines crept unseen down our coastline, taking stations from Halifax to Miami to the Gulf of Mexico.

They were type VII-C U-boats; powerful 740-ton craft that could do 17 knots on the surface, eight submerged. Each carried 14 newly developed electrically propelled torpedoes which couldn't be spotted or dodged because they left no wake of air bubbles. In addition, the U-boats bore guns large enough to sink most merchantmen by shellfire alone, and carried veteran crews skilled in both surface and undersea combat.

Admiral Doenitz unleashed his raiders on 12 January, with the radioed code message *Paufenschlag* (Beat on the kettle-drums). That same day saw the sinking of a freighter south of Halifax, a tanker within sight of Cape Hatteras, and a steamer off Cape Cod. In the next two days, three tankers were torpedoed, and six ships were sunk the following day.

This was the beginning of what Nazi submariners called "the happy time"—the six months during which they met no effective opposition as they sank 382 ships off our shores, often within sight of land. They were all vessels bound for England with cargoes of food or arms and ammunition or diesel oil and gaso-line. They represented a total loss of 3 million tons of desperately needed shipping, which was far more tonnage than our ship-yards could replace in the same period of time. Yet during the entire six-month kettledrum offensive we sank only eight U-boats —a mere 10-day output for Germany's shipyards!

Small wonder, then, that General of the Army George C. Marshall warned the Navy that "the losses to submarines off our Atlantic seaboard and in the Caribbean now threaten the entire war effort . . ."

Operation *Paufenschlag*'s success is easily explained. The Atlantic Fleet's major ships, from destroyers to battlewagons, couldn't be spared from the submarine-infested transatlantic sea-lanes. And all the Navy had left to guard our coastal shipping was a pitifully weak anti-submarine flotilla made up of only three 110-foot and two 173-foot patrol craft, vintage 1929, plus 20 small wooden World War I subchasers! True, the Navy hastily recruited the few available Coast Guard cutters, as well as a number of fishing vessels and pleasure yachts. Even so, the enlarged flotilla was still a "Hooligan's Navy" whose ships for the most part were too feeble to handle a tough 220-foot U-boat. As for antisubmarine aircraft, in the beginning the Navy, without any planes on the east coast capable of ferreting out U-boats far at sea, had to turn to the Army for help—and the Army only had nine planes available for the job!

That we were totally unprepared for *Paufenschlag* is as obvious as the Navy's shortsightedness now seems. For in its frantic effort to build a two-ocean fleet the Navy had been concentrating on the construction of large combat ships and neglecting vessels designed for ASW or antisubmarine warfare. Similarly, it had been ignoring long-range ASW patrol planes in favor of carrier aircraft.

Fortunately, at about the time the kettledrum offensive began Adm. Ernest J. King became commander in chief, United States Navy. A stern old seadog who was more respected than liked, King nevertheless was one of the ablest officers our Navy has ever known. And it was he who reshaped the Navy's building program when, in March 1942, he demanded "60 ASW ships in 60 days," and actually got 67 by 4 May, when another 60-60 program was launched.

What King got were subchasers that had radar "eyes" and sonar "ears" and were armed with "hedgehogs" as well as depth charges. Hedgehogs, a British invention, fired a broad spread of from 8 to 24 shells that went off only on contact. Depth charges, on the other hand, exploded at a determined depth, whether they hit anything or not—a weakness exploited by U-boat commanders, who often fooled their attackers by releasing diesel oil, garbage, and fake wreckage when they were unsuccessfully depth-charged.

Admiral King demanded, in addition, a stepped-up production of twin-engine Catalinas (PBY's), and other long-range radar-equipped bombing planes as well as a more intensive training of pilots in ASW techniques. He borrowed destroyers from the

Canadians and the British, and took a long gamble when he said, he "robbed ocean convoys of escorts to reinforce our coastal areas." With a canny eye to the future, he also ordered our shipyards to hasten the production of two newly designed vessels. One was a small destroyer-escort (DE) that lacked a full-sized destroyer's combat capabilities but was still well enough armed to handle submarines. The other was an escort carrier (CVE) that could be mass produced from merchant hulls. Called "baby flattops" or "jeep" carriers, once in operation they would be able to carry about 20 ASW aircraft into waters beyond the 900-mile range of our land-based patrol planes.

In the summer of 1942 these measures began to pay off, for by then the Navy had enough escort vessels to form an interlocking coastal convoy network, and enough Catalinas and Liberators to fly patrols over the convoy routes. Faced at last with an effective search-and-attack system, Admiral Doenitz shrewdly changed his strategy. Leaving only a handful of subs to harass our seaboard shipping, in August he opened a new U-boat blitz in a section of the mid-Atlantic that quickly became known as the "Black Pit."

The Black Pit was that expanse of the ocean to the north of the Azores that lay beyond the reach of Allied patrol planes, whether they flew out of Newfoundland, Iceland, or the British Isles. Convoys had always been vulnerable there, and they became doubly so with the tactics Doenitz used in his new blitz. He formed "wolf packs" of from 10 to 20 U-boats each, and then established two picket lines of lurking packs to catch convoys coming and going. As for a pack's individual tactics, only a couple of U-boats would attack at first, to draw away some of the escort ships encircling a convoy. Then the rest of the pack would slip through the gap in the broken circle and strike the convoy at close range.

When the main arena of the Battle of the Atlantic shifted to mid-ocean the British, American, and Canadian navies quickly combined ASW forces. But even so the wolf packs were so diffi-

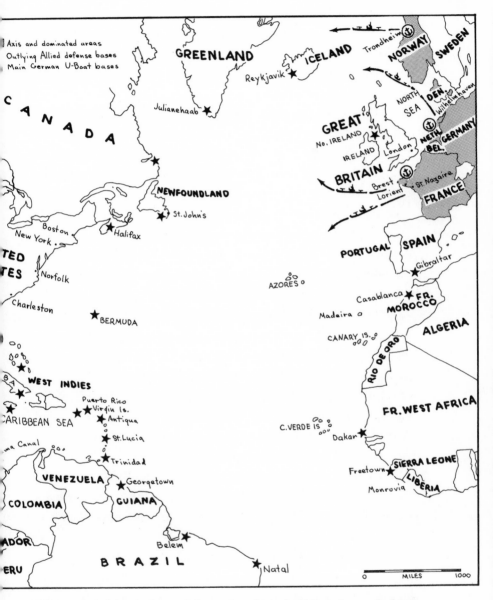

The central Atlantic beyond the range of our land-based patrol planes was the stalking ground of German submarines. Among the merchant convoys sailing almost unprotected through these waters north of the Azores, the region became known as "the black pit."

cult to beat back that they continued to hold the upper hand for eight months. In August 1942, for instance, the packs claimed 102 merchantmen. And in the following five months they continued sinking ships faster than we could replace them, as they averaged better than a vessel a day for a rough total of 2.5 million tons of shipping.

In those grim months it seemed that Doenitz might prevent us from ever ferrying enough men and weapons across the Atlantic to defeat Germany. He was so dangerously close to his goal, in fact, that when Roosevelt and Churchill and their combined Chiefs of Staff met in January 1943, they decided that for the time being their chief objective had to be "the defeat of the U-boat," since if that failed so would everything else. With this decided, the U.S. immediately placed a "Triple-A" priority on the building of DE's, CVE's, and ASW aircraft, no matter what the cost in other badly needed combat ships.

Nonetheless, in February the wolf packs sank 63 merchantmen. In March the blood-curdling score rose to 85 ships in the Black Pit, plus another 23 picked off by U-boats roaming the ocean from Norway to the southern tip of Africa, for a total of 625,000 tons. By May, though, the score had shrunk to less than 200,000 tons. In that same month, too, the Allies raised their score to 41 U-boats—more than they had sunk in the previous four months combined!

May, then, marked the turning point in the Battle of the Atlantic, for thereafter Doenitz would begin losing U-boats almost as fast as they could be produced. (In the remaining months of 1943, 186 were sunk as against 192 built.) And thereafter his surviving crews, now haunted as never before by the prospect of death in the ocean depths, would begin to grow noticeably hesitant in pressing home their attacks.

Facing up to the bitter prospect of ultimate defeat, in June the admiral started to withdraw his wolf packs from the Black Pit. Many of his undersea raiders were then sent into the Indian

A Nazi submarine in the Atlantic Convoy Lanes under attack by planes from the escort carrier Bogue.

A surfaced Nazi submarine after it had been hit by ash can dropped by escort carrier planes.

Escort carrier planes circle the large slick where a Nazi submarine sank. The wake marks of the sub lead up to the spot where it eventually went under.

Ocean and other distant waters where there were as yet no convoys. However, he always kept enough in European waters to send out on hit-and-run raids that continued to give the Allies many anxious hours. Thus the U-boat remained a menace until Germany surrendered. But after 1943 the Allies were so much in control of the main transatlantic sea lanes that they were never again threatened with the loss of more shipping than they could produce, or an inability to transport abroad the troops needed to bring about Hitler's eventual downfall—and this of course spelt victory in the Battle of the Atlantic.

Doenitz believed that submarine warfare is as much a battle of scientific wits as of firepower, and after the war he blamed his defeat on radar, saying that "next to the atomic bomb it was the most decisive single weapon of the war." It was a feeble alibi because the Germans used radar too. But in the radar battle of wits they couldn't keep pace with the Allies. So Doenitz would have come nearer the truth if he'd said that he lost because Nazi scientists were no match for those opposing them.

In the case of radar sets, for example, the ones we originally installed on our search planes operated on a meter-long wavelength. With them, Allied planes could pick up at a range of about 20 miles a U-boat that had surfaced at night to recharge its batteries. Then they could home in on the unsuspecting sub, dive through the darkness, suddenly switch on their searchlights, and release a lethal hail of bombs on its gleaming deck. As a countermeasure, German scientists developed a warning radar that could detect an approaching plane's meter-length radar when it was still 10 miles away, thereby giving a U-boat time to dive to safety.

When we found that our long-wave radars were no longer effective, our scientists quickly developed microwave sets to replace them. And since the Nazis never could figure out how to detect or jam it, the microwave radar deserves credit for a large number of the many U-boat kills made by aircraft after the spring of 1943.

As another case in point, the Germans invented a long-range acoustic torpedo that was guided by "ears" which reacted to underwater sounds. Fired from several miles astern a target, on nearing a ship the torpedo would "hear" its thrashing propellers and swerve directly into them. In theory it seemed an unbeatable weapon. But in practice our scientists easily outwitted it with a noisemaker that our ships towed astern in U-boat waters. Called a "Foxer," the device was simply a cluster of metal rods which clanged together so noisily when towed that they drew in an acoustical torpedo and caused it to explode harmlessly.

Since in most other technological aspects of submarine warfare the story was much the same, it's clear that our superiority in this field played a leading role in reducing the U-boat's effectiveness. But in combat terms, it is generally agreed that our best ASW weapons were the numerous Hunter-Killer Groups the Navy formed in the summer and fall of 1943, after the "Triple-A" priority on DE's and CVE's bore fruit.

Hunter-Killer Groups were made up of baby flattops, each screened by three or four DE's or destroyers (DD's) which were equipped with the last word in sonar, hedgehogs, and depth charges, as well as conventional arms. The carriers' air groups consisted of Wildcat fighters (F4F's) and Avenger (TBF) bombers. The fighters were needed to strafe surfaced U-boats, which in the last years of the war mounted antiaircraft guns. The bombers carried depth bombs or aerial versions of the Nazi acoustical torpedo, called "Fidos," that could smell out a not too deeply submerged target.

The planes also had a scouting radius of about 300 miles, which was important because experience had shown that a mere "air umbrella" over a convoy gave it much less protection than a far-ranging air search of its flanks. Equally helpful in detecting distant U-boats was the high-frequency direction-finder—called "huff-duff"—aboard each ship in a Hunter-Killer Group. With huff-duff the sputter of U-boat radio transmissions, as they sent messages to each other or to Doenitz, could be picked up and plotted. And the groups were of course free to pursue submarines wherever huff-duff fixes indicated their presence.

Hunter-Killer Groups made their kills in one of three ways. Many were made by planes alone. Often, though, a U-boat would spot incoming planes in time to dive out of their reach. Then the planes would coach a DE or DD to the scene. If the escort vessel could make sonar contact with the sub it would hunt the U-boat down and, hopefully, either sink it with depth charges or, as was sometimes the case, damage it so badly that it had to come to the surface and duel for its life in open combat. One such duel was as swashbuckling as it was unique, because for the first time in naval history since the days of sail it was settled by hand-to-hand and man-to-man fighting.

The prelude to the encounter was the radar-sighting by a night-flying pilot off CVE *Block Island* of the surfaced *U-66,* in the moonlit morning hours of 6 May 1944. While the pilot stalked the sub, he coached in the destroyer-escort *Buckley.* She opened fire at long range with a round that holed *U-66*'s conning tower. Now unable to dive, the sub tried to run away. But with *Buckley*'s 35-knot speed it was no contest.

As he bore down on the sub the DE's captain elected to ram it—a not uncommon practice—and cut it in two. But at the moment of impact a wave lifted his bow over the *U-66*'s forecastle, leaving the two vessels locked in a deadly embrace, one atop the other. With this, Nazi seamen erupted from the sub's hatches, some with revolvers in hand, and began scrambling up the DE's sides.

Over the *Buckley*'s loudspeaker a command then rang out that her skipper, a young lawyer turned reserve officer, could only have learned from reading of earlier wars—"Stand by to repel boarders!" But since few of his crew were wearing their

service issue .45's, the question was, With what? Luckily, someone remembered that the ship carried a store of hand grenades,
and a party of men rushed below to break them out.

Meanwhile, those who had .45's emptied them into the first
wave of Nazis to reach the deck, while their comrades searched
for any makeshift weapon they could lay hands on. A Negro
mess boy knocked one German back over the side with a well-
aimed coffee mug. A barrage of empty shell cases floored others.
In the bow, a burly quartermaster slugged it out with three of
the boarders, knocking them all cold. A husky gunner's mate
literally hammered five enemy sailors to the deck with a claw
hammer. And some of *Buckley*'s men simply picked up their foe
and threw them overboard.

Then the hand grenades were passed up a hatch. Few of the
crew had ever seen these soldiers' weapons, but having played
baseball they all knew how to throw them—and did so with a
lethal accuracy that soon drove the boarders over the side. Then
they turned their attention to the *U-66*, with its invitingly open
hatches. Two grenades went down the engine-room hatch, starting raging fires below. Another landed on the conning tower
bridge with an explosive flash that left it covered with shattered
bodies.

But to her credit, *U-66* fought to the last. Reversing engines, she
managed to scrape clear of the *Buckley*. Then, charging back,
she made a dying attempt to ram the DE's thin hull. She struck
it only a glancing blow, though, and with this failure limped off
to go down sizzling, with flames soaring through her open
hatches. After picking up 36 survivors, *Buckley* took count of her
own heads and found she'd suffered but a single casualty. The
hard-slugging quartermaster had a broken knuckle.

Four weeks later, a veteran commanding a Hunter-Killer
Group struck perhaps the decisive blow of the U-boat war when
he gave an order that hadn't been heard in the U.S. Navy in 129
years. It was "Away all boarding parties!"—the exact opposite

of the order given the previous month by *Buckley*'s young skipper.

The veteran was Capt. Dan Gallery, of CVE *Guadalcanal*. Having long dreamed of capturing a U-boat—complete with its codes, engineering secrets and crew—he had had his DE's train parties to board one if the opportunity arose. It came on 4 June 1944 off the bulge of Africa, when DE *Chatelain*'s sonar detected a submerged sub. The contact was reported and seconds later planes roared off *Guadalcanal*'s flight deck.

From the air the pilots, who could see the sub (*U-505*) traveling just below the surface, sprayed the water with machine-gun fire to mark the spot for *Chatelain*. She in turn dropped a pattern of depth charges that rolled the sub on its beam ends and holed its outer hull. Panic-stricken, some of the Nazis screamed, "We're sinking!" Taking their word for it, the *U-505*'s skipper surfaced. Then, finding himself under the guns of three DE's, he ordered the sub's scuttling valves opened.

Anticipating the scuttling attempt, Gallery ordered his boarding parties away the moment *U-505* broke water. Men armed with sub-machine guns piled into whaleboats and raced for the sub, knowing it might sink in a matter of minutes. As they drew near their guns spoke, and all the Nazis who weren't hit dove into the water. The boarders then scrambled onto the abandoned hull and rushed to the conning tower. They could see that the sub was settling rapidly. And every man who climbed down the conning tower knew that the U-boat might plunge to the bottom at any moment. But down they all went, into the dark interior of a ship where the only sound was the frightening gurgle of inrushing water.

In line with their training, some waded through the rising water to the radio room to search for code books. Others hunted frantically for the valves that closed the open sea cocks. And a gunner's mate named Burr probed the darkness with a flashlight as he searched for the 14 time bombs and booby traps known to be hidden in every U-boat. Burr's perilous assignment was to find and defuse these explosive charges.

By Gallery's estimate, *U-505* was no more than a minute away from taking its final dive when the last sea cock was closed. As for Burr, he won a Navy Cross for finding and disarming 13 booby traps. But the 14th remained a terrifying threat until Gallery personally ferreted it out and disarmed it. That done, the captain had the sub towed to Bermuda, where he gleefully demanded an official receipt for "One Nazi U-boat, No. 505, complete with spare parts."

No. 505 was the first foreign warship boarded and captured by U.S. Navy seamen since 1815. It was taken by men as heroic as any sailor who ever flourished a cutlass. And they captured perhaps the most valuable booty the Navy has ever seized. For in their panic the Nazis had violated a basic principle of warfare. They hadn't destroyed their intelligence material before surrendering. Instead, as Captain Gallery says, "Everything was intact—code books, cipher machines, charts of the English Channel mine fields, all tactical instructions for submarines . . . It was the greatest intelligence windfall of the U-boat war.

"The most remarkable part of this fantastic business was the fact that the Germans never found out that we had captured the *U-505*. After the war we learned that she had been listed as sunk, just like all the others that failed to return. So the Nazis continued to use the codes we'd taken off the *U-505*, and we read every single order they sent out to their U-boats. This was the main reason for our high rate of sinkings during the last year of the war."

At this point, with their every move known to the Allies, the U-boats lost their striking power and, except for minor skirmishes the Battle of the Atlantic was over. And having seen how Admiral Doenitz's fangs were pulled, this too is the point to shift our attention back to the other side of the world.

CHAPTER 4

✠✠✠✠✠✠✠✠✠✠✠✠✠

The Victory Disease

We left the Pacific with the situation as black as the smoke still rising from the wreckage of Pearl Harbor. For as President Roosevelt had told Congress on 8 December 1941, "Yesterday the Japanese Government also launched an attack against Malaya . . . the Philippine Islands . . . Guam . . . Hong Kong . . . [and] Wake Island."

It is roughly 7,000 miles from Pearl Harbor to Singapore, in Malaya. Simultaneous attacks launched across so broad a front could have only one meaning; that the belligerent Tojo meant, if possible, to drive all "foreign imperialists" out of the Far East. And with our Pacific Fleet too crippled even to limp into action, it was easily possible.

By the end of December 1941, the Japanese had taken Wake and Guam from us, and Hong Kong from Great Britain. They had overrun Britain's Gilbert Islands, south of the Marshalls, and begun converting the group's main island, Tarawa, into an island fortress. It was obvious by then, too, that all of Malaya—including Singapore, England's "Gibraltar of the East"—would soon fall into the enemy's hands. Oil-rich Borneo, held jointly by the British and Dutch, was invaded on 17 December, securing for Japan much of the petroleum she so badly needed. And invaded Thailand surrendered without a fight.

In the Philippines the Emperor's warriors encountered stiffer resistance. Yet even there the Allied cause was hopeless. On Pearl

Harbor day, Jap bombers from Formosa (Taiwan) had caught all of our planes neatly lined up on the airfields around Manila and destroyed most of them. With the Japanese in control of the skies, our weak Asiatic Squadron—two old cruisers, 13 destroyers and a few auxiliary vessels—had to abandon its base in Manila Harbor. Then the enemy made nine amphibious landings and surrounded the combined U.S. and native armies of the Philippines, commanded by Gen. Douglas MacArthur. Manila fell on 27 December. And later, when it was clear that the Philippines were doomed, Roosevelt ordered MacArthur to Australia, where he was to take command of the U.S. troops being sent to that subcontinent to meet the onrushing Japs.

Within a month Tojo had come close to realizing his dream of conquering East Asia. But he still had to win the Malay Barrier, the name then given to the arc of islands, mostly held by the Dutch, running from the tip of the Malay Peninsula to New Guinea. The main islands—Java, Sumatra, Bali, and Timor— were rich in oil, rubber and other raw materials needed by Japan's war machine. And the straits between them were waterways through which the enemy could descend on Australia.

Although the British, Dutch, Americans, and Australians joined forces to defend the Malay Barrier the story never varied; always greatly outnumbered, they were always defeated, and in the opening months of 1942 the Barrier fell to the Japs. At the same time Tojo, with forces to spare, reached out for Lae and Salamaua, side-by-side ports on New Guinea's northern shore, and for New Britain, Bougainville, and New Ireland, the three northernmost islands of the Bismarck Archipelago. This shrewd move placed the Japanese so close to Australia's naval base at Darwin that it had to be abandoned. The move also allowed the enemy to build a major base at one of the world's finest harbors, Rabaul in New Britain. And with the seizure of Lae-Salamaua the Nipponese were within close striking distance of Port Moresby on New Guinea's south coast, an ideal springboard from which to launch an invasion of Australia.

Finally, to protect his western flank against a possible assault from India, Tojo sent an expeditionary force into the Bay of Bengal to seize the Andaman Islands and Burma's chief seaport, Rangoon. With this, the enemy was in control of all of East Asia except inland China.

A line drawn on a map from Wake to Tarawa, then across to Rabaul and Lae-Salamaua, ending with an arc that encompasses the Malay Barrier and stops at Rangoon, shows the amazing extent of Japan's early conquests. In addition to establishing a far-reaching defensive perimeter studded with formidable bases she had in the short space of five months brought under her sway over 300 million square miles of oceans and islands!

"Never before in military history was so much gained for so little cost, in such an incredibly short time," according to an American admiral. In fairness, he should have added that seldom before has one nation's armed might been so overwhelmingly superior to that of its foes.

At the outbreak of war in the Far East the combined surface forces of the Allies amounted to only 2 battleships, 9 cruisers, 24 destroyers, and a few gunboats—and the two battleships, England's *Prince of Wales* and *Repulse*, were trapped and sunk by Jap torpedo planes in the first 72 hours of fighting. Opposing this feeble force were 4 battleships, 24 cruisers, 61 destroyers, 10 carriers, and hundreds of transports carrying hundreds of thousands of invasion troops, all brilliantly maneuvered by Tojo's naval genius, Fleet Admiral Isoroku Yamamoto. In the air, Yamamoto had 750 carrier planes and the support of 2,000 land-based planes. The Allies, with no carriers, had 713 land-based planes, none a match for the enemy's swift, agile carrier fighter, the Zeke.

Considering the odds, that the campaign made military history of a sort is hardly surprising. At sea the Allies fought heroically in a series of battles whose names—Java Sea, Badung Strait,

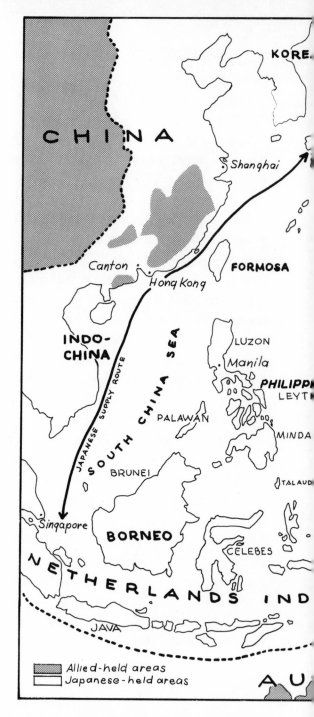

Within five months of the Pearl Harbor attack, the Japanese held sway over 300 million square miles of the Pacific Ocean and the resources of

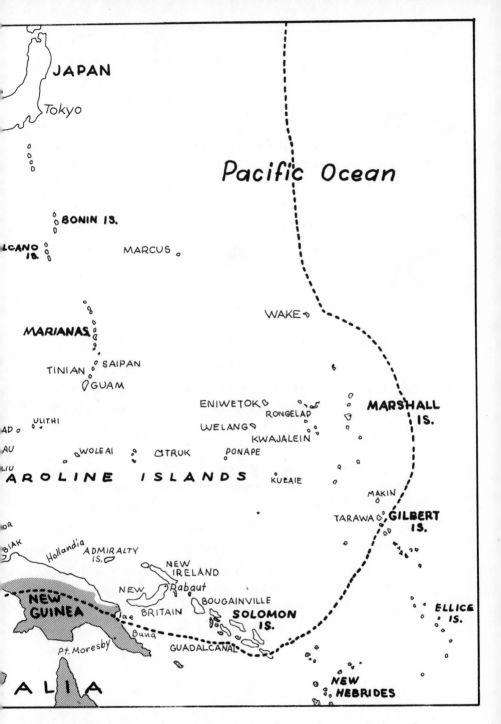

its wealthy islands. Never in history had such gains been made in such
a brief period with so little cost to the attacker.

Balikpapan—fall strangely on our ears. On land, too, Allied troops fought bravely with what little they had. But with his superior forces the enemy would simply seize a strategic point with the help of a carrier striking force, build an airfield, soften up his next objective with bombing from both land and sea, occupy it with a carrier-escorted amphibious force, then move on to his next objective.

Inevitably, in the end the Allies lost most of their planes, ships, and land forces—at the incredibly small cost to the Japanese of only three destroyers and equally insignificant air and ground losses! Ironically, though, in crushing the Allies the enemy had for the first time demonstrated to the world the almost limitless offensive capability of something new to naval warfare—the fast carrier striking force. And in so doing the Imperial Navy not only set the pattern for the Pacific War but also set the stage for its own defeat! For as it turned out, Japan's downfall was, to a large degree, brought about by the improvements we subsequently made in the carrier tactics first used by the enemy.

Charged with not having adequately defended Pearl Harbor —many think unfairly in view of the misleading intelligence sent him from Washington—Admiral Kimmel was relieved as commander in chief, Pacific Fleet (Cincpac) at the end of 1941. His successor was Adm. Chester Nimitz, a kindly, quiet, white-haired Texan. As a commander, naval historian Samuel E. Morison says, Nimitz "had the leadership to weld a great fighting team, the courage to take necessary risks, and the wisdom to select from a variety of intelligence and opinions the correct strategy to defeat Japan."

When Nimitz became Cincpac the ships of his battle line were either sunk or fast in the mud. To offset Yamamoto's 10 carriers he had only *Enterprise* and *Lexington* (*Saratoga* was still in the repair yard), plus the knowledge that two of the Atlantic

Fleet's four carriers—*Hornet* and *Yorktown*—would soon join the thin line of ships steaming through the Panama Canal to reinforce him. It would be a year and a half, though, before any of the new battleships and carriers under construction could come to his aid.

While his immediate prospects were as dismal as his fleet was lean and the enemy's was fat, Nimitz still made good use of what little he had. Unable to mount a major attack, he sent carriers out to harass the enemy in a series of bold hit-and-run raids. The raids were merely feints and counterblows, like the left jabs of a boxer who is trying to keep a heavier opponent off-balance. Yet one jab so angered the enemy that he tried to retaliate with a knockout punch—and missed so badly that it changed the entire nature of the Pacific War.

Shaggy, tough Adm. William "Bull" Halsey threw the first jab when he led *Enterprise,* screened by three cruisers and six destroyers, in a raid on the Marshall Islands in February 1942. Concentrating on Kwajalein, the Jap's main base, his planes sank a transport, damaged nine ships, and killed the base commander.

Even more daring was one of the raids made the following month, when a task force built around *Lexington* and *Yorktown* crept through the poorly chartered Coral Sea into the Gulf of Papua on New Guinea's south coast. There the force lay in the shadow of the 2½-mile-high Owen Stanley mountain range, whose permanently cloud-capped peaks had never been mapped. The range seemed to form an impenetrable barrier between the task force and Lae-Salamaua, 150 miles away on New Guinea's north shore. But according to intelligence reports, there was a narrow pass somewhere in the mountains, only 7,500 feet high and usually free of clouds in the morning hours.

Scout planes found the pass on 9 March, and the following morning 103 planes poured through the mountain slot and swooped down on Lae-Salamaua. A cruiser, two destroyers and five cargo vessels were sunk, and six warships listed as "probably sunk." The enemy, caught flatfooted, knocked down one dive-bomber.

The left jab that had such far-reaching consequences came in April. It was a raid on Japan's capital, Tokyo, by 16 B-25 twin-engine Army bombers launched from the *Hornet*'s flight deck at a point only 668 miles off the coast of Japan. The B-25's had been borrowed from the Army because no carrier bombers had the range to operate outside the limit of the Japanese offshore air patrol. Their Army pilots, led by Col. James Doolittle, had been specially trained in carrier takeoffs. But since no carrier deck was long enough to recover the big planes, the plan called for them to end their flight in then friendly China, as all but three did.

The raid was Admiral King's idea. He knew of course that a mere 16-plane strike would do Tokyo little damage. But he also knew that something as spectacular as a raid of this nature was needed to lift the morale of the American people who were deeply depressed by Japan's unbroken string of victories. And the news of the raid did in fact give the American public the boost in spirits King had anticipated.

What no one anticipated, though, was the Imperial High Command's reaction to the raid. As a Japanese admiral said later, his country's high-ranking officers had all caught "the Victory Disease." Having conquered the Far East without a single defeat, they had grown so conceited that they thought themselves invincible and their homeland untouchable. Consequently, the bombing of their beloved capital was more than their victory-diseased egos could bear. To them it was a humiliating slap in the face that simply had to be answered. So they struck back with what was meant to be a knockout blow, and blundered instead into a military error known as "strategic overstretch."

Instead of wisely consolidating their recent conquests, as they had planned, they now decided to reach out for still more territory. First, Port Moresby and the Solomon Islands would be seized to secure control of the Coral Sea gateway to Australia. Then Yamamoto and his combined fleet would cross the Central Pacific, destroy our Pacific Fleet, and at the same time capture Midway Island and occupy Alaska's Aleutian Islands. After that, New Caledonia, the Fijis, and Samoa would be invaded. Australia would then be isolated. Midway-based bombers would be within reach of Pearl Harbor. And the entire Pacific from Alaska to Australia, from Tokyo to Hawaii, would be a Japanese lake!

The only truly sound part of the overambitious plan was Yamamoto's challenge to the Pacific Fleet. A wise old sea lord, Yamamoto knew that if our fleet was ever to be annihilated it had to be before 1943, when our shipyards would begin replacing the Pearl Harbor losses. He knew too that we would have to meet his challenge because Midway, Nimitz' last defensive base in the Pacific and only remaining "sentry for Hawaii," had to be defended at all costs. With his immense superiority, Yamamoto naturally expected to win. And he hoped that after another crushing defeat the American people, sick and tired of a losing war, would force their Government to quit and leave the Pacific to Japan.

That was the plan and the hope and the expectation. But as an Imperial Navy officer wrote later, "We were so accustomed to success that no thought was given to the possibility that things might not go exactly as planned." And yet there never was a possibility that things would go exactly as planned, because through superb intelligence work Nimitz had learned of the enemy's intentions. He knew that before forcing his hand at Midway the Japanese planned to invade both Port Moresby and Tulagi, a good harbor on a small island opposite Guadalcanal, in the Solomons. And being forewarned, Nimitz hurriedly united what few ships he had in the South Pacific into Task Force 17 and sent them into the Coral Sea to stop the enemy.

Task Force 17 consisted of *Lexington* and *Yorktown,* 10 cruisers and 11 destroyers. The Japanese invasion force had almost twice as many warships defending its troop transports, as well as air support from carriers *Shoho* and two Pearl Harbor veterans, *Shokaku* and *Zuikaku.* And, between them, the opposing fleets blundered through a notably mistake-filled encounter, which perhaps was to be expected because the Battle of the Coral Sea was the first naval engagement in history in which aircraft carriers alone decided the issue, without a shot being fired by a surface ship.

The Japanese won the first round when they took Tulagi unopposed, by virtue of having beaten TF 17 to their objective by a day. In a sense they won the second round, too, because when *Yorktown*'s planes bombed Tulagi harbor 24 hours later, they scored scarcely a hit. But because of foolish penny-pinching, the enemy at the same time missed a chance to strike back. To save the cost of an extra plane-ferrying trip, battlebound *Shokaku* and *Zuikaku* had stopped off at Rabaul to deliver nine fighter planes, with the result that they were too far away to go after *Yorktown!*

For the following two days the rival task forces searched for each other without success, though at one time only 70 miles separated them. Then at dawn on 7 May a Jap plane spotted a fueling unit retiring from TF 17—and mistakenly reported the oiler and its escort destroyer to be a carrier and a cruiser! Scenting blood, *Shokaku* and *Zuikaku* launched their air groups, sank the helpless small ships—and missed an opportunity to attack our carriers with their decks empty.

For at the same time our planes were also on a wild-goose chase after "two carriers and four cruisers" seen by a *Yorktown* search plane. Not until TF 17's flights were airborne was the report corrected to "two cruisers and two destroyers." But as luck would have it, in mid-flight our fliers sighted carrier *Shoho.* Swarming in, they put her under in 10 minutes and radioed back the famous words "Scratch one flattop," the phrase that later became standard for reporting the death of a carrier.

After three days of blind fumbling, on 8 May the carrier groups finally located each other. It was as even as a match could be; two flattops versus two, 121 enemy planes against our 122. The weather, however, favored the Japanese, because a heavy squall blotted out *Zuikaku*. Seeing only *Shokaku*, our fliers tore her upper decks apart with three solidly planted bombs. Our carriers, both bathed in sunlight, were attacked simultaneously. And although the fighters flying combat air patrol over our force took a heavy toll of the Jap planes, particularly those from *Zuikaku, Yorktown* took a bomb that caused considerable damage and *Lexington* was hard hit by two torpedoes and two bombs. At first *Lexington*'s damage control parties thought they could save her. But eventually she was so gutted by internal explosions that her captain had to order her abandoned.

The USS Lexington *after the "abandon ship" had been ordered, 8 May 1942.*

While waiting for rescuing destroyers to come alongside many of the crew of "Lady Lex," as they called her, displayed a memorable, if feigned, nonchalance. Braving the below-deck fires and explosions, they salvaged the two-gallon cans of ice cream in the ship's canteen, and even remembered to bring topside a supply of wooden spoons and paper cups. Then, refreshments in hand, they calmly waited in line to go over the side into waiting rescue craft. Later, though, their true feelings surfaced. Most of them wept unashamedly as they watched their beloved ship quietly slide beneath the water with a dignity that moved one of her officers to say, "She was a lady to the end."

Although we'd lost *Lexington*, nevertheless the Japanese commander decided to throw in the sponge. With *Shoho* sunk, *Shokaku* too badly damaged to launch planes, and *Zuikaku*'s aircraft losses heavy, he simply didn't have enough air cover left to protect his Port Moresby invasion force. So he had to order his fleet to retire to Rabaul.

For the enemy the Battle of the Coral Sea was a tactical victory. He had taken Tulagi, and in terms of tonnage sunk he was also the victor. But for our Navy it was an important strategic victory. Never again would the Japanese be able to remount their Port Moresby invasion force. And since it took two months to repair *Shokaku* and a month to replace *Zuikaku*'s plane and pilot losses, neither carrier could join in the great battle coming up. But *Yorktown* could and did. When she limped into Pearl Harbor on 27 May, by Nimitz' orders 1,400 workmen repaired her bomb damage in two days, instead of the 90 that had been estimated!

Nimitz *had* to have *Yorktown*, because the old saying, "Forewarned is forearmed," didn't hold for him. He was forewarned because he'd learned from intercepted and deciphered radio messages that the two-pronged attack on the Aleutians and Midway was scheduled for the first week in June. But he was by no means forearmed.

Yamamoto was taking to sea 86 warships, the largest armada the Imperial Navy had ever assembled. To challenge him, Nimitz had less than half as many—42. And of his fighting ships, 6 cruisers and 11 destroyers were wasted in a North Pacific Force whose commander let the enemy's Aleutian Invasion Force slip by him and take Attu and Kiska islands without a shot being fired. (Ironically, the Japs found the islands so strategically unimportant that when a U.S. Army unit eventually retook Attu the Japanese in turn evacuated Kiska because they didn't consider it worth fighting for.)

Thus for Midway Nimitz had left only 8 cruisers, 14 destroyers, and 3 carriers. But in Rear Adm. Raymond Spruance, of the *Enterprise-Hornet* task force, and Rear Adm. Frank Fletcher of the *Yorktown* group, he had brilliant commanders. And he had Midway itself, to which he sent all the planes the tiny island would hold; 115 bombers and fighters.

Yamamoto took to Midway 5 carriers, 9 battleships, 10 cruisers, and 56 destroyers, divided into: (1) an occupation force of well-protected troop transports approaching the island from the south; (2) a striking force of four heavily screened carriers, led by Admiral Nagumo, moving in from the north; and (3) his own main force of seven battleships and a screen that included a light carrier, lurking behind Nagumo's ships. Yamamoto hoped that his main force would not be spotted until he brought up his battleships to finish off the U.S. warships Nagumo's planes failed to sink.

Not knowing their plot had been uncovered, the Japanese were counting heavily on the element of surprise. They figured that it would take two days for our small fleet to reach Midway from Hawaii, that this would give their occupation force time to capture Midway, and that they would then be free to deal with our ships. As for air opposition, they didn't expect much, what with *Lexington* sunk and *Yorktown*—they thought—knocked out of action. That they might be sailing into a cleverly laid ambush, that Nimitz might have a task force waiting for them northeast of Midway never seriously entered their minds.

Hidden by the dense clouds of a foul-weather front, Nagumo's striking force reached Midway just before sunrise on 4 June, unseen by any of the island's anxiously searching patrol planes. At dawn, 108 of his planes took off for the island. Also launched were the fighter-plane combat air patrols (CAP's) carriers always send aloft as sentries. And spotted on the flight decks of the four carriers—Pearl Harbor veterans *Akagi, Kaga, Hiryu,* and *Soryu*—were 93 planes armed with torpedoes and bombs designed for use against ships; a conventional precaution should any enemy war craft appear unexpectedly.

At Midway, all of the island's planes were in the air minutes after radar picked up the incoming air strike; the fighters to defend the island, the bombers to counterattack. There were far too few fighters to stop the attackers. Even so, about 30 of the enemy were downed and the rest, while they did considerable damage, were driven off before they knocked out the island's runways. Meanwhile our bombers were suffering heavy losses and scoring no hits. Yet futile as their attack was, it led Nagumo into a fatal error.

At 7 o'clock he had heard from his strike commander that Midway needed another working over. Nagumo had a choice. He could wait 90 minutes for his returning planes, rearm them, and send them back. Or he could take immediate action by ordering his 93 reserve planes below to their hangar decks to be rearmed with bombs suitable for use against the island. He was still debating his choice when our Midway bombers came in sight and made up his mind for him. He saw them as evidence that Midway might hurt him if he didn't bomb it again quickly. So he decided to rearm his reserve planes at once—and the decision cost him the battle.

For the ambush had already been sprung. At 6 o'clock a search plane had sighted and reported the enemy carriers' position to Fletcher and Spruance. Both knew that Nagumo's striking force was "Yamamoto's jugular vein" and that it had to be cut at any cost. They shrewdly guessed that Nagumo would have to strike Midway twice, and that he would continue heading toward the island in order to improve his position for recovering planes. They also figured out that by 9:15 Nagumo's flight decks should be crowded with recovered planes being refueled and rearmed. And since this is the moment when carriers are most vulnerable, they timed their launchings accordingly. At 8 o'clock, when they were 175 miles from the enemy's calculated position, *Hornet* and *Enterprise* sent off 116 planes. Just in case more targets were found, 35 *Yorktown* planes were held back for an hour. Then they too were sent winging.

Nagumo had long since learned that he'd fallen into a trap, for only 15 minutes after he'd sent his reserve planes below a Jap scout plane had reported "10 enemy ships" to the northeast, instead of in Pearl Harbor where they were supposed to be. Nagumo, completely dumbfounded, wasted 15 minutes trying to decide what to do. Finally he cancelled his switch-bombs plan and ordered his reserve planes again rearmed to attack ships.

Removing bombs and installing torpedoes takes a long time, however, and before it could be done Nagumo had lost his only chance to launch 93 planes against our carriers. He was forced, instead, to keep his flight decks clear to recover the planes returning from Midway. The first landed at 8:35, the last at 9:06. Only then did the striking force turn eastnortheast "to contact and destroy the enemy." And just as Fletcher and Spruance had figured, Nagumo's flight decks were jammed with planes being rearmed and refueled in frantic haste.

Because of the change in course *Hornet*'s fighters and dive-bombers missed their target. But *Hornet*'s 15-plane torpedo squadron, led by Lt. Comdr. John Waldron, sighted Nagumo's ships. The squadron was eight miles from the nearest carrier. Anti-aircraft shells were already reaching out for it. The dreaded

Zekes of the enemy's CAP were hurtling toward the 15 planes by the dozen. And the squadron hadn't a single fighter to protect its slow, lumbering aircraft. But Waldron and his men did have one thing—a raw courage unsurpassed in naval history.

Diving full throttle, they leveled out just above the water and, against hopeless odds, headed straight into a gantlet of bursting shells and deadly accurate Zeke machine-gun fire. Waldron and his rear gunner went first, in flames. Then, one by one by one, the 14 planes following him came to the same fiery end. None ever got close enough to drop their torpedoes. Of the 30 men in the squadron, only one survived.

Within 15 minutes the *Enterprise*'s 14-plane squadron attempted a similar and equally courageous attack. It too had accidentally become separated from its fighter protection. Yet without a moment's hesitation the squadron tried to bore through a swarm of Zekes, in a heroic effort to get within range of *Kaga*. Ten planes were shot down. Few got close enough to release their torpedoes. None scored a hit.

Then it was *Yorktown's* turn. Her 12 planes had 6 Wildcat (F4F) fighters covering them. But the Wildcats were easily tamed by the faster, more maneuverable Zekes. Then 10 of the 12 torpedo planes fell to the Zekes, too, five after dropping torpedoes that never found a target.

The massacre ended at 10:24. Thirty-five of 41 torpedo planes had been lost. Not a torpedo had found its mark. And for about two jubilant minutes the Japanese were sure they had won the battle.

But our torpedo squadrons had not sacrificed themselves in vain. On the contrary, it was their martyrdom that cleared the way for our victory. For they had drawn down from high in the sky the Zeke CAP's that otherwise would have been waiting to pounce on our dive bombers. And in six dramatic minutes our dive-bombers completely reversed the tide of battle. So as the Japanese historian of Midway says, "The Americans succeeded largely because after engaging their torpedo planes our fighters had not yet had time to regain altitude to meet their dive-bombers."

At 10:26, Comdr. Clarence McCluskey, flying at 14,000 feet, brought two squadrons (38 planes) of *Enterprise* dive-bombers in over Nagumo's carriers. Selecting *Kaga* as his target, McCluskey ordered one squadron to follow him, the other to head for *Akagi,* Nagumo's flagship. With no Zekes to harry them, the two squadrons plummeted down for the kill. *Kaga,* with 30 fueled and armed planes on her flight deck, took four hits, became a blazing inferno, and sank following a violent internal explosion. *Akagi* received a bomb that set off the torpedoes in the planes on her hangar deck, another that exploded in the midst of her 40 topside planes. His flaming flagship ob-

A Japanese heavy cruiser lies dead in the water after having been bombed by carrier planes at the Battle of Midway.

viously mortally wounded, Nagumo transferred to cruiser *Nagara,* then ordered *Akagi* sunk by a destroyer's torpedo.

With two carriers accounted for, *Yorktown*'s dive-bombers arrived just in the time to catch *Soryu* turning into the wind to launch planes, and planted three half-ton bombs in their midst. Turned into a blazing bonfire, *Soryu*'s flames weren't extinguished until a prowling U.S. submarine, *Nautilus,* sent her 2,600-fathoms deep with a torpedo salvo.

Thus at 10:30 the Japanese, who had been certain of victory at 10:24, found themselves with three big carriers in their flaming death throes. There was still *Hiryu,* though, and at noon Nagumo ordered her attack group to strike *Yorktown.* Of the 40-plane group that found *Yorktown* at 2:45, only seven broke through our CAP and antiaircraft fire. But that was enough. Three dive-bombers got hits, as did two of four torpedo planes. Badly hurt, *Yorktown* developed such a sharp list that Fletcher had to transfer his flag to cruiser *Astoria.* Taken in tow by a destroyer, *Yorktown* was inching homeward when a Jap sub, *I-168,* put an end to her.

But *Yorktown* was soon avenged, for at 5 o'clock the *Enterprise*'s planes found and downed *Hiryu* with four direct hits. And that was it. Where there had been four big carriers there were now none.

That our fliers sank one of Nagumo's heavy cruisers and badly damaged another the following day doesn't alter the fact that the glorious Battle of Midway was won on 4 June 1942, in one of the most sudden reversals of fortune in the history of warfare. And Yamamoto knew it, because when he learned that his "jugular vein" had been cut he muttered, "Enough is enough." and ordered his fleet to retire. Then, shattered by his loss, he took to his bed for a week with "his face ashen and his eyes glazed," according to an eyewitness.

He had lost his entire fast carrier group, along with 253 planes and pilots and about 2,200 officers and seamen. We had lost

Yorktown and 109 carrier planes, many of whose pilots were saved. But what probably sickened Yamamoto even more than the cold statistics was the blow to his and to Japan's pride—a blow so severe that it caused Tojo to ban even the mention of the name Midway at Imperial headquarters. For under Yamamoto's command the Japanese Navy had suffered its first defeat in its 250-year existence!

To the Japanese the consequences of the battle were disastrous. The limits of their expansion in the Far East had been reached. Port Moresby, New Caledonia, Fiji, and Samoa were now beyond their grasp. Midway remained a strong American outpost. And in six explosive minutes the Imperial Navy had lost its overwhelming superiority.

True, with the aircraft carrier now the dominant warship, their navy, with five carriers fit for action, still held a slight numerical edge over the Pacific Fleet's three large carriers. But the edge would soon be dulled, since Japan's shipyards were incapable of keeping pace with ours. Indeed, on 4 June, Japan had only six carriers on the stocks or under repair, while we had 13 large and 15 escort carriers abuilding.

Thus the Battle of Midway changed the whole course of the Pacific War, because following the destruction of Nagumo's carriers the balance of power in the Pacific shifted steadily to our side. So from Midway onward Japan was condemned to fight a largely defensive war. And Admiral Nimitz could say with quiet satisfaction, "Well, Pearl Harbor has been partially avenged."

CHAPTER 5

✲✲✲✲✲✲✲✲✲✲✲✲✲

Beginning With
a Shoestring

Although Admiral King supported the strategy of defeating Germany first he was also determined to mount an offensive in the Pacific as soon as circumstances permitted. Not to do so would leave the Japanese free to strengthen their outer defensive perimeter at their leisure and, given time, they might make it almost impenetrable. So after Midway, King began arguing his case before the Allied Joint Chiefs of Staff. He could not have picked a worse time. The Allies were building up their forces for an invasion of North Africa and had little manpower or equipment to spare for other theaters of war, as the British heatedly pointed out. But King persisted and finally won approval for Operation *Watchtower*—the code name given our first offensive campaign in the Pacific.

Its target was the Bismarck Barrier, formed by the Solomon Islands and the two islands of the Bismarck Archipelago, New Britain, and New Ireland. These islands are so close to one another that planes flying from them can control thousands of miles of neighboring waters, and in Japanese hands they completely blocked the ocean roads leading north from Australia to Tokyo. At the barrier's northwestern end the foe was already entrenched in Rabaul. He had bases on Bougainville in the middle of the barrier. And at its southeastern end he was beginning to dig in at Tulagi. Obviously, we had to breach the Bismarck Barrier if we were ever to advance northward from Australia.

Watchtower called first for the capture of Tulagi and a landing on nearby Guadalcanal, still unoccupied according to intelligence reports. From these islands we would then advance to Bougainville on Rabaul's eastern flank. As a second step, once we had a foothold in the Solomons, General MacArthur would advance up New Guinea's Papuan Peninsula to Lae-Salamaua, to outflank Rabaul from the southwest. Finally, the two advances would converge on Rabaul and wipe out Japan's chief stronghold in the Southwest Pacific. A gateway to Tokyo would then be open.

On 5 July, just three days after *Watchtower* was approved, Nimitz held a conference with the officers he'd chosen to lead the Tulagi-Guadalcanal phase of the operation. One was Admiral Fletcher, commanding the Expeditionary Force centered around *Enterprise, Saratoga,* and *Wasp,* a carrier newly arrived from the Atlantic Fleet. The other was Adm. Richmond Turner, commander of the Amphibious Force.

The three flag officers felt uneasy about *Watchtower,* and with reason. Despite its recent losses the Imperial Navy still had us outgunned and outnumbered, and with more carriers could still put more planes in the air. There were also large air wings at Rabaul. This meant that the enemy would be in control of the air and able to pound us unmercifully while we were building airstrips on Guadalcanal and flying in the air groups needed to neutralize his air supremacy.

In addition, the Imperial Navy would be operating from bases that were close at hand, whereas our advance bases in the South Pacific—Espiritu Santo Island and Noumea, in New Caledonia—were about a thousand miles from Guadalcanal. Geography favored the enemy in another respect too, because the Slot—the narrow channel separating the two strands of islands in the Solomons group—begins at Bougainville and ends

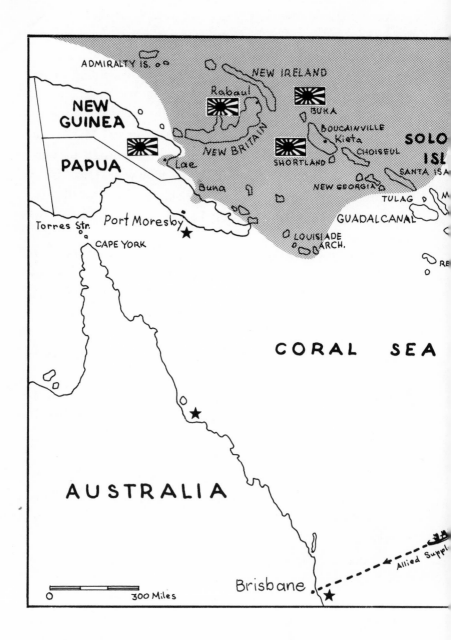

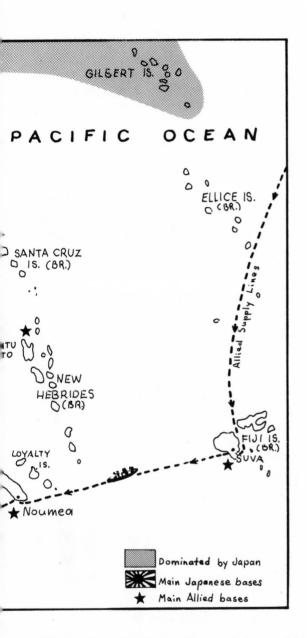

The capture of Guadalcanal in the Solomon Islands was essential to protect Allied supply routes and prevent the isolation of Australia. The landings were carried out in the face of superior Japanese naval forces.

at Guadalcanal. Thus troops that had been convoyed from Rabaul to Bougainville could then be ferried down a land-locked passageway, under a shield of land-based planes, to attack our Guadalcanal beachhead.

Time was also a factor, because the landings were scheduled for early fall, which gave the three admirals an uncomfortably short period in which to plan and organize an operation as complex as an amphibious assault. And how about our assault troops; the 1st Marine Division, then stationed in Fiji? Guadalcanal, 90 miles long and 25 wide, was a rain-soaked, malaria-infested jungle island. In their sweep through the Pacific the Japanese had gained the reputation of being unbeatable in jungle warfare. Could our untested Marines stand up to the foe's jungle veterans?

Finally, there was the question of reinforcements and supplies. With the invasion of North Africa having top priority for everything, these would be hard to come by. Yet they would certainly be needed, because the enemy's reserves at Rabaul far outnumbered the 19,000-man 1st Marines. Nor could MacArthur help, since as yet he had a mere three divisions with which to conduct phase two of *Watchtower*. So the only answer was a most unsatisfactory one. All of our Pacific bases would have to be stripped of the majority of their men and supplies to back up the Marines.

Everything considered, it's not surprising that the trio of admirals nicknamed the venture Operation *Shoestring*. Then, to add to their worries, at the end of their conference they received a jolting message—one of our patrol planes had spotted an airfield under construction on Guadalcanal! This made launching *Watchtower/Shoestring* even more urgent, so much so that D-day was advanced to 7 August. Capturing the airstrip before the Japs could finish it was a must, because victory might well depend on who first put it into operation.

In mid-July there was more news. The Japanese had landed

at Buna-Gona, on the Papuan Peninsula directly across from Port Moresby. While this was worrisome to MacArthur, it was encouraging news to Cincpac. If Rabaul's attention was focused on its perennial target in New Guinea, there was a chance Guadalcanal could be taken by surprise.

On 26 July, Fletcher's warships rendezvoused off Fiji with the Amphibious Force transporting Maj. Gen. Alexander Vandegrift and his 1st Marines. Before dawn on 7 August the invaders slipped past the volcanic cone of Savo Island and entered Savo Sound—the small body of water separating Guadalcanal and Tulagi, soon to become the graveyard of so many ships that it was renamed Ironbottom Sound.

The surprise was complete. The unfinished airstrip at Lunga Point—later christened Henderson Field in memory of a Marine pilot killed at Midway—was in the hands of the Leathernecks by late afternoon, so slight was the opposition from Guadalcanal's 2,000-man garrison. The seaplane base at Tulagi, though more stoutly defended, was secured the following morning. For a shoestring effort, it all seemed easy.

But Adm. Gunichi Mikawa, commander, Outer South Seas Force, had already left Rabaul and was heading toward the Slot with seven cruisers and a destroyer. He knew he couldn't reach Guadalcanal in time to deny us a beachhead. But knowing the strategic value of the Bismarck Barrier, he intended to fight for every inch of it. And on his arrival, shortly after midnight on 9 August, in 30 savage minutes he gave the U.S. Navy the worst licking it has ever taken in a fair battle—with the help of some unpardonable blunders by our side.

Fletcher made the first mistake when he took his carriers away to refuel beyond reach of air attack, even though he was by no means critically short of fuel. As a result, during the waning hours of 8 August none of his planes was flying air searches over the Slot and Mikawa's approach wasn't detected. Even so, the screening force, left to cover the operation, had no excuse for being caught as flatfooted as it was.

Two destroyers were on picket duty at the mouth of the Slot. And the entrances into Savo Sound from the Slot—the channels to the north and south of Savo Island—were guarded by heavy cruisers. Yet Mikawa somehow slipped past the picketing destroyers. Then he catapulted three seaplanes to reconnoiter our cruisers and drop flares to illuminate targets for his gunners. To track our ships' moves, his planes had to fly so low that they were visible to our cruiser captains. And, incredibly, they all made the same fatal mistake—they all assumed that the planes were friendly!

Guided by his eyes in the sky, Mikawa steamed to within a mile of the two cruisers and lone destroyer patrolling the south channel before launching torpedoes. With precise timing, his seaplanes waited until the torpedoes were near the end of their runs, then dropped flares. At the same moment Mikawa's seven cruisers opened fire. The nearest ship, floodlighted by the flares, was *Canberra,* one of two Australian cruisers enlisted to strengthen the shoestring operation. Bearing the brunt of the attack, in less than a minute *Canberra* was literally blasted apart by two torpedos and 24 eight-inch shells. Astern of her U.S.S. *Chicago,* hit only by a single shell and a torpedo that notched her bow, turned tail to the enemy cruisers and took off after Mikawa's lone destroyer. Whether she ran out of cowardice or in confusion no one knows, because her captain later committed suicide.

Intent on bigger game, Mikawa sped past *Chicago,* rounded Savo Island, and fell on the three heavy cruisers guarding the north channel. They too were caught flatfooted, because *Chicago* had not sent out a warning and *Canberra* hadn't had time to. So Mikawa's flagship, *Chokai,* was able to account for *Astoria* singlehandedly, with rapid-fire salvos that turned her into a blazing, sinking hulk in a matter of moments. With the same expert marksmanship, the rest of the Japanese squadron concentrated on *Vincennes* and *Quincy,* sinking them only minutes apart.

Now Mikawa made his only mistake. Not knowing our carrier bombers were too far away to threaten him, he broke off the action for fear of being caught by them at dawn. Had he been a gambler, he could easily have sunk most of our transports and supply ships at anchor off Lunga Point. Still, as he sped back up the Slot he could gloat over a great victory. In half an hour he had killed 1,270 seamen, wounded 709, and sunk four heavy cruisers—to begin the steel paving of Ironbottom Sound.

With its shoestring frayed to the breaking point, for the time being the Navy had no choice. To avoid further losses it had to order all ships to retreat to distant Noumea. About 16,000 Marines—who would soon explode the myth that the Japanese were unbeatable in jungle warfare—had been landed. But the departing ships still held half of their weapons and supplies. So they were left facing a dismal prospect; that of holding on to their beachhead and converting Henderson Field into a usable airstrip with far less than they needed for the job, and then waiting—waiting for the supplies and reinforcements that had to be forthcoming if they were to survive.

As General Vandegrift summed it up, "It was to be expected that the Japanese reaction at sea and in the air would be violent. It was, and because the enemy was able to bring heavy air and naval concentration to bear in the area, our own air and surface forces had to act with utmost caution.

"In the early days ashore we had no coastal artillery, and Henderson Field had no planes. Supplies could not be brought in often enough to meet our needs . . . [and] we were seriously short of weapons.

"The ability of the Japanese to bring in reinforcements and to pound our positions from both air and sea resulted in recurring crises ashore. During the first four months, fighting rose each month to a climax in which a fresh and determined enemy force strove to push us into the sea. Slashed and repulsed, the enemy withdrew each time to gird for another try with replenished man-power and supplies. Meanwhile, we were unable to take the offensive because we lacked sufficient combat troops to drive inland and guard the airfield at the same time.

"In mid-October, after some planes had joined us, our aviation gasoline reserves fell desperately low. Then, following a heavy enemy assault, ammunition became pure gold. Food problems forced us to settle for two meals a day. But before another major attack broke, heroic efforts by naval forces brought sufficient relief to see us through.

"American seamen and airmen, outnumbered and outgunned, had begun to gain the upper hand with their superior skill, courage, and equipment. In time, they could pour fresh ground troops into the island at will . . ."

As Vandegrift suggests, the Navy's task was in its own way as difficult as that of the Marines. Even more badly outmatched after the Battle of Savo Island than in the beginning, in the following three months the Navy suffered additional serious losses. Yet in those months it still managed to get enough reinforcements and supplies through to enable the hard-pressed Marines to hang on. But try as it might, it couldn't interrupt the flow of fresh troops, and weapons poured into the island by the enemy.

They were carried by what we called the Tokyo Express, an almost nightly dash down the Slot by troop-laden destroyers and light cruisers to Japanese-held beaches, where the Express discharged its cargo, then hurried back before daybreak to its staging areas in the upper Solomons. On runs involving less than a thousand men, air coverage and the Express' own guns were considered sufficient protection. But for the protection of super-Express runs convoying large numbers of troops, the enemy usually deployed a carrier task force to ward off any ships we might send in to the attack.

The first super-Express run was made in late August. We tried to attack it but failed, because our force, spearheaded by *Saratoga* and *Enterprise,* had to contend instead with the three-carrier interception group defending the convoy. In the air battle that developed, our bombers sank the light carrier *Ryujo.* But the enemy's planes got through to *Enterprise* and splintered her flight deck so badly that she had to return briefly to Pearl Harbor for repairs. Worse still, while *Saratoga* was retiring from the action, she took a torpedo from a submarine that put her in drydock for three months.

This left us with only two working carriers, *Hornet* and *Wasp.* And in September, while they were convoying the 7th Marine Regiment to Vandegrift's aid, we were sent reeling by yet another blow. A submarine penetrated *Wasp*'s destroyer screen and ended her life with three torpedoes. But with the Marines fighting with their backs to the sea there could be no turning aside, so

The carrier Wasp *in flames after being hit by three enemy torpedoes near Guadalcanal, 15 September 1942.*

the transports and *Hornet*—now our only operational flattop—
pushed on and landed the regiment.

In October, with four carriers on hand to fence with *Hornet,*
the Japanese showed their contempt for our waning air power
by adding battleships and heavy cruisers to the Tokyo Express.
Confidently cruising close inshore, on three successive nights these
warships mauled Henderson Field with more than 2,500 14- and
8-inch shells, leaving in their wake many dead Marines, a pockmarked airstrip, 48 shattered planes, and the field's supply of
aviation gas in flames.

At this point Admiral Nimitz frankly admitted, "It now ap-
pears that we are unable to control the sea in the Guadalcanal
area . . . The situation is not hopeless, but it is certainly
critical . . . so critical it calls for a more aggressive commander." Then he named as commander in chief, South Pacific,
a pugnacious seadog who fought his best when the odds were
against him, "Bull" Halsey. At this point, too, President Roosevelt bluntly told the British that we were going to reinforce
Guadalcanal and do it quickly—even if it meant drawing from
the forces being assembled to invade North Africa.

Before help could reach the island, however, the Japanese
made their strongest attack yet on Henderson Field, feeling
certain that this time they couldn't be stopped. The Tokyo
Express had just added 4,500 men to their island garrison. They
thought their naval bombardment had thoroughly softened up
our beachhead. And at sea they had the biggest armada Yamamoto had assembled since Midway, with orders to "annihilate
any forces or reinforcements approaching the Solomons area."

And again their onslaught failed. On land it was turned back
by the supposedly softened-up defenders of Henderson Field,
who for a week (19–26 October) fought so fiercely that the
enemy finally had to retire to replenish his badly shot-up forces.

At sea, the Combined Fleet of 63 major warships and four
carriers was aching for a fight. And it got one, even though

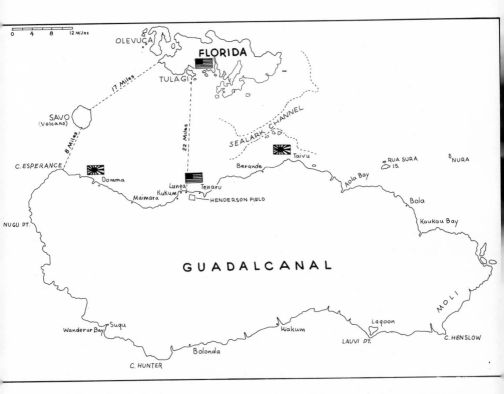

Tulagi Harbor and Henderson airfield were the vital areas to control in the conquest of Guadalcanal. The small body of water between the two points, nicknamed "Ironbottom Sound" was the scene of one of the U.S. Navy's worst defeats and also one of its splendid victories.

Halsey had only *Hornet, Enterprise* (fresh from the repairyard), and 21 screening vessels. But for him it was enough, and when he dispatched his slim force his orders to its tactical commander, Rear Adm. Thomas Kinkaid, were as brief as they were blunt— "Attack—repeat—attack!"

The David-and-Goliath encounter began when two of our scout planes located Nagumo's flattops on the morning of 26 October. The planes were carrying 500-pound bombs "just in case." And with matchless courage, after reporting the enemy's position the two lonely dive-bombers braved the combined fleet's massed antiaircraft fire, to plant their bombs on light carrier *Zuiho* and knock her out of action in the battle's first moment—and then escaped to tell their story!

After that it was a free-for-all, with opposing air groups actually passing within sight of each other, and each wondering if it would have a flight deck waiting for it on its return. As fate (in the form of six bombs and three torpedoes) would have it, this day ended *Hornet*'s notable career. *Enterprise* was hit again too, though not so badly that she couldn't take aboard both her own pilots and those from *Hornet,* when they returned to report that, while they had missed carriers *Junyo* and *Zuikaku,* their missiles had torn *Shokaku*'s decks to shreds and left a heavy cruiser and two destroyers in bad shape. Furthermore, when last seen the Combined Fleet was northward bound, away from the arena.

Since the loss of *Hornet* reduced our Pacific carrier strength to *Saratoga* (in dry dock) and *Enterprise* (in need of minor repairs), it might seem that the Japanese had triumphed. But *Zuiho* was temporarily crippled. *Shokaku* was out of the war for nine important months, being repaired. The enemy had lost 112 veteran pilots, half of them to the withering fire of three of our new antiaircraft cruisers, while only 20 of our planes had been shot down. And because so many of the enemy's lost pilots were from *Zuikaku,* she too was out of the war for the weeks it took her to pick up and train a new air group. So in

A Japanese bomber descends in flames after taking a direct hit from the guns of the USS Hornet.

reality this was the battle in which our Navy, in Vandegrift's words, "began to gain the upper hand."

Most important of all, though, was the fact that with the land assault having failed and Kinkaid having turned back a fleet that by rights should have crushed him, we had gained just enough time to prepare for the next crisis, the climax of the campaign for Guadalcanal.

In the opening days of our hard-won grace period, the first of Roosevelt's promised reinforcements arrived. Vandegrift got a few infantry battalions, two artillery units, and fresh squadrons of Marine combat planes. Halsey got another new modern battleship, *Washington,* to pair with *South Dakota.* In addition, 6,000 troops were loading aboard seven transports that were due at Guadalcanal in mid-November.

It was a desperate race against the clock, though, because in the same period the Tokyo Express unloaded 65 destroyer and two cruiser loads of troops. And according to our scout plane reports, 40 warships and 20 transports were about to sortie from the Rabaul area. For the South Pacific Fleet this was ominous news. Now in addition to protecting a seven-transport convoy it would also have to beat back the enemy's strongest amphibious thrust of the entire campaign, which had obviously been beefed-up with an eye to overpowering any naval force we could bring together.

Acting on intelligence estimates that the enemy's invasion force would reach Guadalcanal about the 15th of November, we rushed our transports to Lunga Point on the 11th, hoping to get them unloaded and away before shells began to fly. Accompanying the transports was an escort of cruisers and destroyers, under Rear Adm. Daniel Callaghan. Halsey also had available *Enterprise, Washington, South Dakota,* and their screen, with Kinkaid on *Enterprise* and Rear Adm. Willis Lee commanding the battleships. These ships were waiting in Noumea for the repairmen to finish with *Enterprise.* But to be on hand for the battle

A Navy scout observation plane.

expected on the 15th they finally had to weigh anchor with welders and riveters still aboard the carrier, working round the clock.

Then on the afternoon of the 12th, when our transports were about 80 percent unloaded, the unexpected happened. Search planes sighted 2 battleships and at least 4 cruisers and 10 destroyers boiling down the Slot at a speed that would bring them into Ironbottom Sound after nightfall. Since no troopships were sighted. it was clear that the enemy was out to attack our transports and bombard our shore positions. It was equally clear that Callaghan and his five cruisers and eight destroyers were no match for the enemy force. Yet with our carrier-battleship group still too far away to help, he had no choice. Pulling our transports out, he escorted them to safety, then returned to Ironbottom Sound to face what seemed certain annihilation.

On a moonless night, Callaghan reentered the Sound shortly after midnight with his ships in single column—four destroyers in the van, followed by cruisers *Atlanta,* his flagship *San Francisco, Portland, Helena* and *Juneau,* and four destroyers bringing up the rear. At 1:24 a.m. his radar picked up Vice Adm. Hirokai Abe's ships, 13 miles off his port bow. Callaghan could have turned broadside to the enemy to bring more of his guns to bear. But if he had, he would have come under the fire of the 14-inch guns of the battleships *Hiei* and *Kirishima* long before his smaller guns could reply. So he chose instead to plunge headlong into the middle of a Japanese formation that could throw three times more metal per salvo than his ships could.

Admiral Abe was the first to open fire, following his discovery that Callaghan's lead destroyers were penetrating his formation. Then began a fierce, indescribably confused free-for-all. For in the inky blackness of the night it was difficult to tell friend from foe. To try to identify a dimly seen silhouette with the help of a battle searchlight was to invite destruction—to have heavy metal scream back through the searchlight's beams to their source. And for a ship to attempt to establish its own identity with blinking code lights was equally hazardous. Thus with the two forces meeting head-on and vessels having to veer sharply to avoid collisions or turn abruptly to dodge torpedoes, all battle order was soon lost. No tactical maneuvering was possible. Instead the action became a wild melee in which individual ships milled around firing at targets of opportunity, which sometimes turned out to be friendly.

The scene was as wild as the fighting. Torpedoes crisscrossed the sea. Red smoke trails of tracer shells cross-stitched the sky. Geysers of white water erupted as shells missed their mark. Blinding orange flames flared briefly when they struck home. The cannonading, Marines ashore said later, was louder than thunder. Black smoke spewing from oil-fed fires made the dark sky even darker. And in time the horizon became dotted with the dull red glow of abandoned hulls and the yellow torches of ships still ablaze.

"The most savage fleet action of modern times," as it's been called, raged for 38 minutes. It took place, ironically, on a Friday the 13th. And it ended with all but one of our ships shot up. Four destroyers were either sunk or sinking, two were tangled masses of metal topside, one had lost only her foremast, but the eighth, miraculously, wasn't even scratched. Cruiser *Atlanta*'s fires were out of control, her scuttling inevitable. *San Francisco* and *Portland*, though badly holed, could still fire, as could *Helena*, whose injuries were minor. *Juneau*, her spine broken by a torpedo, was creeping along at snail's pace. And the force's commanding officer was now Captain G. C. Hoover, of *Helena*. Admiral Callaghan had ordered his flagship to "take on one of the big ones," and in engaging battleship *Hiei* he and his staff had been killed by a 14-inch salvo.

It was as lame a force as would limp away from any engagement of the war, yet a victorious one. For in the face of the reckless fury of its charge, the Japanese had turned tail, so demoralized and confused that some of their ships were firing on each other as they withdrew. Moreover, Admiral Abe retreated with a force that was still much stronger than the one Admiral Callaghan had led into the fray; the battleship *Kirishima* and 14 other ships. All he left behind was one sunken destroyer, another with its engines shot to pieces, and *Hiei,* dead in the water from 85 hits and destined to be sunk after daybreak by bombers from Henderson Field.

Abe had failed utterly, and because of his timidity Yamamoto relieved him of his command. But in death Admiral Callaghan had fulfilled his mission. He had saved Henderson Field from a disastrous bombardment that would have, among other things, halted its air operations—which in the next 24 hours accounted for 11 enemy troop transports.

At dawn Captain Hoover ordered all ships that could still move to join up with him. Of Callaghan's original 13 vessels only *San Francisco, Juneau* and three destroyers could obey. *Portland* had to ignore the order because, although she was moving, a torpedo hit had jammed her rudder in such a way that she could only turn in circles. But her guns were still manned. And when daybreak revealed the remaining enemy destroyer, dead in the water six miles way, *Portland* sank her with six salvos, fired one to a turn—a feat that Nimitz called "one of the highlights of the action." *Portland*'s pride in her marksmanship was soon dampened, though, by a Jap submarine which in mid-morning sank *Juneau* with most of her crew, to bring to an end the first round of the naval Battle of Guadalcanal.

Despite Abe's defeat the tactical situation on the 13th still favored the enemy. Hoover's cripples of necessity had to retire to Espiritu Santo. And our carrier-battleship task force was still far to the south. This left the defense of Guadalcanal in the hands of a few PT boats and the Marine air group at Henderson Field. Knowing from their air searches that we had no surface ships in the area, the Japanese now tried to regain the initiative.

They slipped two heavy cruisers into Ironbottom Sound in the dark morning hours of the 14th. And at the same time a super-Tokyo Express of 11 destroyers and 11 large transports started down the Slot on a bold schedule that called for it to disembark troops in broad daylight.

The cruisers spent a busy hour in the Sound, with half their batteries trained on Henderson Field, half on a swarm of PT boats. They managed to ward off the torpedo boats and succeeded in blowing up 18 planes and some supply dumps on the airfield, before vanishing into the night in hopes of evading our morning air search. But in midday, Marine pilots found and holed them both. And then some *Enterprise* planes appeared overhead. They had been launched at extreme range to fly into Henderson Field and beef-up its air strength and were almost out of gas. Nevertheless they paused long enough to sink heavy cruiser *Kinugasa* before continuing on—with an anxious eye to their fuel gauges.

At Guadalcanal they learned that the super-Express had been sighted and that Marine planes were already en route to the attack. After refueling and rearming, the *Enterprise* group sped off to join the fray. Between them, the two air groups either sank or gutted by fire 7 of the 11 approaching transports. The other four, though hit, pressed on until their bows were on the beach, where they too were eventually destroyed by air raids that also took a heavy toll of their troops.

Meanwhile another night action was in the making. To give Henderson Field some surface ship support, Admiral Kinkaid had detached *Washington* and *South Dakota* and four destroyers from *Enterprise*'s screen, with orders to sprint ahead to Ironbottom Sound. This placed our ablest battleship commander, Admiral Lee, on a collision course with Adm. N. Kondo, who was also speeding toward the Sound. Kondo had 13 cruisers and destroyers and the battleship *Kirishima,* which he had picked up from the retreating Abe. His mission was to do what Abe had failed to do—tear apart Henderson Field and all of its

planes, so that a second fleet of transports bearing down on
Guadalcanal could land its troops.

Lee entered the Sound shortly before midnight on the 14th,
and his radar failed at first to reveal any trace of opposition. But
he was immediately picked up and reported to Kondo by a light
cruiser of the enemy's advance screen. Kondo at once ordered
his main force to come to full speed. Lee then spotted the light
cruiser, fired at her, and missed. As she turned to run, Lee's
four destroyers went after her—and ran into an ambush. Two
Japanese destroyers were steaming so close to the shore of Savo
Island that radar could not distinguish them from the land mass.
Lurking there unseen, they unleased fan-shaped spreads of torpedoes that sank *Preston* and *Walke* and left Lee's other two
destroyers wallowing.

With only two battleships, Lee continued to head for Kondo's
14-ship task force. Then, with the range closing and *Washington's*
turrets swinging to bear on *Kirishima, South Dakota* suffered
an electric power failure! With steering control lost and her
turrets frozen in place, she was useless as a fighting machine. But
as an unwilling decoy she played an important role in the conflict.
For when destroyer *Ayanami's* searchlight illuminated *South Dakota,* her obvious helplessness made her such a tempting target
that Kondo ordered *Kirishima* to concentrate on her.

And that was a mistake. Because while *Kirishima* was duti-
fully pounding away at *South Dakota, Washington* sneaked up
on the huge Jap battlewagon and at 8,400 yards—short range for
a battleship—rapidly pumped nine 16-inch and 40 five-inch shells
into her. With his command aflame from stem to stern and a
maze of twisted metal topside, *Kirishima's* captain had no choice.
He ordered her scuttled and his men over the side.

Lee then turned his attention—and his guns—to the destroyers
and cruisers that were also concentrating on *South Dakota.* But
as *Washington* closed in on them, firing all the while, *South
Dakota's* electricians managed to restore her power. Then she

got her revenge for the punishment she'd taken. Drawing a bead
on *Ayanami*'s searchlight, she blew the destroyer out of the
water. This loss, added to *Kirishima*'s, was more than Kondo
could stomach. Ordering his remaining 12 ships to retire at
1 o'clock on the morning of the 15th, he left our two battleships alone and triumphant on the oil-and-wreckage-fouled waters
of Ironbottom Sound. And that was the end of the vicious three-
day naval Battle of Guadalcanal.

No one understood the significance of the encounter better
than General Vandegrift, who promptly sent Admiral Halsey
this message:

> The enemy has suffered a crushing defeat. We thank Lee for
> his sturdy effort last night. We thank Kinkaid for his interven-
> tion yesterday . . . But our greatest homage goes to Callaghan
> and the men who with magnificent courage against seemingly
> hopeless odds drove back the first hostile stroke and made suc-
> cess possible. To them the Marines lift their battered helmets
> in deepest admiration.

After its defeat the Imperial Navy urged Tojo to abandon
Guadalcanal as a lost cause. But the stubborn warlord refused to
listen to reason. As a result, the struggle went on for another
three months—but with an entirely different complexion.

We could now ferry in troops at will. By bringing in Navy,
Marine, Army, New Zealand and Australian air groups and
placing them under the command of a gnomelike little man who
proved to be one of the scrappiest flag officers of the war, Rear
Adm. Marc (Pete) Mitscher, we gained control of the air. And
at sea, although we lost two cruisers and had three damaged in
later fighting, we eventually reduced the once dreaded Tokyo
Express to an occasional pathetic rice-train run, with enemy
destroyers striving to get close enough to land to toss overboard
bags of rice that they hoped would float ashore into the hands
of their semistarved garrison.

To make matters worse for the Japanese, by January 1943,

they were in serious trouble in New Guinea, too. Their Buna-Gona beachhead had been wiped out by General MacArthur's troops who were doggedly pushing forward the second phase of Operation *Watchtower*—the advance up the Papuan Peninsula to seize Lae-Salamaua and outflank Rabaul from the southwest. So in late January, Tojo had to give in and order his Guadalcanal garrison withdrawn to man Japanese-held bases in the upper Solomons and to free some of his reserve troops for duty in New Guinea. In a matter of weeks, then, 11,000 men were removed from the island under cover of darkness. Left behind were the sick and the wounded—and the now veteran American jungle fighters who had won the first major ground victory of the Pacific War.

So our shoestring, though at times severely strained, had in the end proved too tough for the foe to break. Rather, we had done the breaking—into the Bismarck Barrier. And this, as Winston Churchill so aptly put it, marked "the end of the beginning" of the Allied offensive to capture Rabaul, drive the enemy out of the Southwest Pacific, and open a road northward to Tokyo.

There is no space in a book of this length to describe the dozens of battles fought during phase two of *Watchtower*. Moreover, although they were all bitterly contested by a trapped and never-surrendering enemy, many were comparatively minor engagements. Even more to the point, much of the fighting was done by foot soldiers whose story logically belongs in an army rather than a naval history. This is particularly true of New Guinea, where the Navy's role was largely limited to bringing supplies to General MacArthur's Australian, New Zealand, and U.S. infantrymen.

In the Solomons, it's true that small Navy units were in almost constant combat. One cruiser task force, for instance, fought 16 engagements in the Slot, all very similar to those fought around Guadalcanal. They were either forays against the Tokyo Express, now running to Japan's outposts in the upper Solomons; or they were bombardment missions, sent out to soften up Ballale, Vila, Munda, Rendova, Bairoko, or one of the numerous other enemy bases Admiral Halsey had to seize to carry out his orders to advance toward Bougainville island-by-island.

Of course, the Navy also had to see that the soldiers assigned to capture each island got ashore safely, and then protect them until their beachhead was securely established. But here again the story of the actual conquest of the islands belongs to the infantryman. A grim story it is too, since it deals with the worst sort of jungle fighting. In the first months of the campaign it is also the story of green, untried troops held to a snail's pace by a more experienced opponent. For example, it took 38,000 men six weeks to wrest the enemy's main airfield in the central Solomons, Munda, from its 8,000-man garrison.

Paradoxically, though, the agonizing slowness of the early ground fighting probably helped shorten the war by several years. At least, it forced us to adopt a new strategy which, as it turned out, not only speeded up the conflict immeasurably but also played havoc with Japan's defensive plan. Indeed, after the war Tojo told General MacArthur that "leapfrogging" was one of the main factors in Japan's defeat.

Originally we had planned to "island-hop" our way to Rabaul as well as to Tokyo. However, it took us three months of hard island-to-island fighting to move a mere 250 miles nearer to Rabaul. Had we continued at that pace, it would have taken 10 years to reach Tokyo. Realizing that the enemy's stubborn resistance and policy of never surrendering might eventually wear us out, the Joint Chiefs of Staff decided to switch from "island hopping" to "leapfrogging."

Leapfrogging was called the strategy of "hitting 'em where they ain't." Enemy strongholds like Rabaul would simply be bypassed. Instead of besieging them, we would seize less strongly defended positions close by, seal the surrounded strongholds off with air and sea power, and leave their garrisons to "wither on the vine."

That was what happened to Rabaul. Halsey leapfrogged up to Bougainville and built there an airfield that was only 300 miles from the enemy's key base. MacArthur jumped from Papua to New Britain's Cape Gloucester, 275 miles west of Rabaul. New Zealand forces took lightly defended Green Island, 120 miles to the east. To complete the encirclement, U.S. Army units then overran the 4,000-man garrison on Manus Island, 400 miles north of Rabaul.

Thus, what started out as a shoestring ended as a strangler's noose. True, the foe's naval units wriggled free of the noose and escaped to Truk (another Japanese island stronghold destined to be leapfrogged) far to the north. But 100,000 of Japan's finest ground fighters were trapped in Rabaul for the duration of the war. The Bismarck Barrier was erased. And our leap to Manus had not only taken us closer to Tokyo but also given us a magnificent landlocked harbor that would become one of our most important staging bases in months to come.

Finally, it should be noted that Fleet Admiral Yamamoto didn't live to see the end of the campaign. At its height, he flew from Rabaul to inspect his forward bases, after first radioing his timetable to his base commanders. Halsey's intelligence officers intercepted and decoded the message, then passed the word to Henderson Field. The plane, carrying Yamamoto, approached Bougainville exactly on schedule—and so did 16 of our fighter planes. The old warrior died in the sky, and apparently with admirable dignity. For when his plane crashed his bullet-ridden body was thrown clear of the wreckage. And when his body was found his hands were still calmly folded over his sword. To the Japanese his loss was one of the war's major setbacks. There was, they said, "only one Yamamoto."

CHAPTER 6
✿✿✿✿✿✿✿✿✿✿✿✿✿

A Torch Is Lighted

The second week in August 1942 was a bad one for the Joint Chiefs of Staff. They were shocked first by the news of the loss of four cruisers to Admiral Mikawa in the battle off Savo Island. And they received another jolt later in the week when they learned of the loss of a single man, on the other side of the globe.

The man was a courier carrying a Top Secret letter from the Joint Chiefs to the governor of Gibraltar. The letter was to let him know that Gen. Dwight Eisenhower would be commander in chief, Operation *Torch* (the invasion of North Africa), and that the general would be directing the assault from Gibraltar, which had a communications center that could keep him in as close touch with Washington and London as with his field commanders.

An outline of the operation was also in the letter. D-day would be 8 November. Three French North African ports would be taken: Oran and Algiers on the Mediterranean, and Casablanca on the Atlantic coast of Morocco. There would be three task forces. The Western Naval Task Force would sail from Norfolk, Va., to attack Casablanca. The others would sortie from England, escorted by the Royal Navy. The Center Naval Task Force would sail against Oran, the Eastern against Algiers. A total of 107,000 troops would be put ashore, all but 23,000 of them American, on beaches whose exact locations were spelled out in the letter.

The jolt to the Joint Chiefs came when the courier's aircraft was shot down by German fighter planes off the coast of Spain. His body was then washed ashore, picked up by Spanish authorities, and eventually turned over to British security officers. Their first concern of course was with the letter, which they found inside the officer's buttoned tunic. It was still sealed and didn't seem to have been tampered with. But because it had been water-soaked no one could be absolutely certain that it hadn't been opened, read, and then resealed.

Yet this was a very real and worrisome possibility. For while Spain was officially neutral it was known that her dictatorial ruler, Franco, favored the cause of Hitler and Mussolini and had given their spies free run of his country. So the crucial question was: Had the friendly Spanish shown the letter to an enemy agent? If they had, the Allies were in trouble. Because if the foe knew all of the details of Operation *Torch,* it would almost certainly end in a military debacle.

The haunting fear that their plot had been uncovered gave our military planners many sleepless nights. Then a British security agent suddenly remembered something that, at the moment, had seemed unimportant to him. When he had unbuttoned the dead courier's tunic, he had dislodged grains of sand as he undid each button. Since the grains had obviously become wedged under the buttons as waves rolled the body ashore, the sand seemed to prove that no one else had unbuttoned the tunic to search the courier's clothing and, it followed, that no one had found or tampered with the letter. It wasn't proof positive, perhaps, but it was enough to quiet the fears of all concerned and let them proceed with their planning with confidence—their path smoothed, paradoxically, by a few grains of abrasive sand.

Opening a front in North Africa was a roundabout way of moving toward a showdown in Europe. But because of the situation in the European theater of war in mid-1942, it was an unavoidable detour. The Germans and Italians held most of the continent and were in a position to control the rest of it, with two exceptions: The British still held Gibraltar, and the Russians continued to hold out against the massive armies that Hitler in his folly insisted on wasting in a campaign that was leading him down the road to disaster.

However, the Nazis still had in reserve more than enough veteran divisions with which to defend the continental beaches bordering the English Channel. On the other hand, in four years of bloody fighting the British Army had been sadly weakened, and only a fraction of America's manpower had as yet been mobilized and trained to a point of combat readiness. So any thought of striking at the Axis by the shortest and most logical route—across the English Channel—was for the time being out of the question.

Obviously, too, beachheads on the European coast of the Mediterranean were for the moment also beyond the Allies' reach. In North Africa, though, the enemy's grip was less firm. At the eastern end of the Mediterranean were Britain's tough Desert Rats, an army operating out of Egypt. Libya, in the center, was both an Italian colony and the base for an Axis army that had been battling the Desert Rats for two years, with neither army ever quite able to conquer the other. To the west of Libya lay two countries—Algeria and Morocco—that the Allies had selected as the enemy's Achilles Heel.

They had been chosen chiefly for two reasons. If we could capture their three main ports we could land the troops and tanks necessary to attack the enemy's African divisions from the rear and, with the help of a frontal assault by the Desert Rats, wipe them out. Then all of North Africa would be in our hands and we would have an ideal springboard from which to launch amphibious attacks on Sicily, Italy, occupied Greece, or southern France—whichever we chose.

There was a possibility, too, that Morocco and Algiers were politically vulnerable. Both were French colonies with no reason to love the Germans. Yet both were ruled by the puppet Vichy government that the Germans had set up to control the unoccupied regions of France, south of Paris. To create the myth that Vichy France was politically independent, the Germans had allowed its government to proclaim itself neutral in the war. And to strengthen the myth the Germans had deliberately not stationed forces in southern France, Algeria, or Morocco. The Nazis were confident that their French puppets would do as they were told, even if it meant ordering their armed forces in North Africa to fight their former allies.

But there was a chance that the Vichy French might welcome their erstwhile allies and join forces with them or perhaps put up only a token resistance. To explore this possibility, U.S. agents talked secretly to Marshal Henri Pétain, head of the puppet state. They hoped to persuade him that our operation was not so much a violation of his government's neutrality as a torch that would eventually light the way to the liberation of all France, and that he therefore should not oppose our landings.

Pétain got the point, but he was afraid of what the Nazis might do if he ordered his North African commanders to lay down their arms. And he was still wavering between our persuasion and his fear of Hitler's revenge when the Western Naval Task Force sailed from Norfolk on 23 October 1942, not knowing whether it would be welcomed ashore or would have to fight its way onto the beaches surrounding Casablanca.

Could they have seen the amount of military hardware and shipping assembled for *Torch,* the men at Guadalcanal would have wept—or cursed—with envy. For example, there were more than 250 ships in the two forces that sailed from England to take Oran and Algiers. And there were another 107 ships in the force which is of chief interest to us because it alone was entirely American in makeup—the Western Task Force.

In the WTF, the ships being convoyed were tankers, cargo ships, 25 transports loaded with 35,000 troops, and a converted

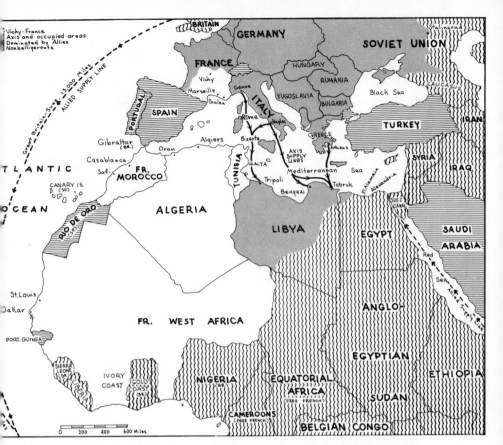

North Africa was the key to the first invasion of the European continent by allied forces. Control of North Africa shortened British supply lines and provided a staging area for assaults against Sicily and Italy.

seatrain carrying 250 tanks. Protecting the convoy were 3 battleships, 5 heavy and 4 light cruisers, more than 40 destroyers, the Atlantic Fleet's only large carrier, *Ranger,* and 4 escort carriers —all commanded by Rear Adm. Kent Hewitt. It was an armada that dotted a 20- by 20-mile spread of ocean. Yet huge as it was, it slipped across the sea without being seen by Nazi submarines. With its electronic HF/DF (huff-duff) eyes, the Navy was able to spot every U-boat then in the Atlantic and set courses that evaded them all. This extraordinary feat not only saved the fleet from torpedo attacks but also kept the Germans from learning what was afoot.

As the force neared the African coast it split into three separate amphibious groups. None, however, headed directly for Casablanca. The large naval base there was protected by heavy 8-inch coast defense batteries. There were submarines, a destroyer squadron, a light cruiser, and a battleship in the harbor. And although the battleship *Jean Bart* was unfinished and unable to get up steam, she was near enough completion to have four working 15-inch guns. And these, coupled with the emplaced 8-inchers, were capable of wrecking an amphibious assault on Casablanca, had we been reckless enough to attempt one.

Instead, our landing groups headed for the flanks of the base. The Northern Group's first objective was the port of Mehedia at the mouth of the Sebou River, 75 miles northwest of Casablanca; its main objective the only year-round airfield in Morocco, nine miles up river at Port Lyautey. The Southern Group's target was Safi, 150 miles southwest of Casablanca; the nearest harbor with water deep enough to allow the seatrain *Lakehurst* to dock and discharge the tanks needed to seize Casablanca by land, as planned. The Center Attack Group set sail for Fedhala, a port on a Cape of the same name, only 12 miles from Casablanca. All three groups would be confronted by shore batteries; none of them, though, as formidable as those at the naval base. The Center Group, in addition, would have to protect its transports from Vichy's warships, should they attack.

As scheduled, at about 5:30 a.m. on D-day, 8 November, the landings began at all three beachheads. And as the first infantrymen scrambled ashore at Cape Fedhala, the question of whether or not the French would fight was answered. The Cape's searchlights suddenly came to life and its shore batteries just as suddenly opened fire. The French were going to give battle. Pétain had issued no orders to the contrary and his Moroccan commanders were keeping their pledge to support his government.

Four destroyers and the cruiser *Brooklyn* immediately closed in on Cape Fedhala to duel with the shore batteries and cover the waves of assault boats speeding ashore. At about 6:30, *Brooklyn* scored a direct hit on a gun in one battery, and moments later knocked out a second battery's fire control mechanism. From the beach, ground troops then began lobbing mortar shells into the concrete emplacements of battery after battery, silencing them one by one. And by mid-afternoon Fedhala was safely in the hands of 7,750 U.S. infantrymen.

Off Casablanca there was a duel too, with the guns of the El Hank battery, close by the harbor lighthouse, and *Jean Bart's* guns challenging those of the battleship *Massachusetts* and the cruisers *Wichita* and *Tuscaloosa*. In short order, five of *Massachusetts's* 16-inch shells silenced *Jean Bart* for the day. It took

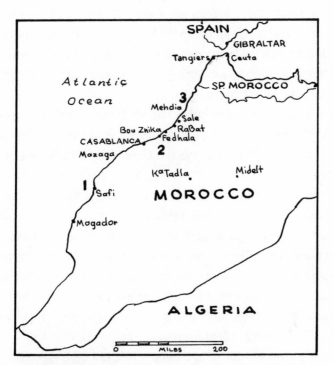

Navy units supported the first attacks in North Africa at (1) Safi, (2) Casablanca, and (3) Mehedia where initial resistance came from French units under orders from the Vichy government.

more time and 175 shells from the cruisers to quiet El Hank.

After the duel ended, at 8:15 in the morning, Vice Adm. François Michelier decided to counterattack with everything he had, and under a smoke-screen cover seven destroyers, eight submarines, and a light cruiser charged out of the harbor toward our transports unloading off Cape Fedhala. (It was learned later that at this hour the admiral and his men still weren't sure who the invaders were and, as one historian says, "didn't much care." They were being attacked, and whether it was by Germans, British or Americans, honor demanded that they fight back.)

Honor, however, seldom carries the day against superior forces, and although the French fought valiantly they were too few and too weak. Our firepower was vastly heavier and our carrier planes ruled the skies. Thus before noon the French could count four destroyers sunk or missing, two destroyers disabled, and a cruiser dead in the water and destined to be sunk later by dive-bombers —a sorry price to pay for hitting a few landing craft and lightly damaging one of our destroyers.

At Safi there was no trouble. The Southern Attack Group had two old destroyers whose superstructures had been removed to make room for 350 assault troops. Guided by a flashlight in the hands of an ensign in a rubber scout boat, these destroyers crept into Safi's narrow harbor under cover of darkness and landed their raiders with ease. The raiders, in turn, as easily chased a company of Foreign Legionnaires out of town. At dawn our carrier pilots neutralized a small airfield nearby. In the afternoon *Lakehurst* began unloading tanks. And by 10 November they were all ashore and ready to roll toward Casablanca.

Mehedia, the Northern Group's first objective, was much tougher. There were 3,500 Moroccan infantrymen in the Kasba, a fortress at the mouth of the Sebou River. Fighting with grim determination, these native soldiers held out until the afternoon of the 10th, before surrendering to the U.S. Army units besieging them.

At daybreak on the morning of the 10th, though, the Kasba's 5-inch guns were still firing, and for a while they had an extraordinary target. It was the destroyer-transport *Dallas,* gallantly bent on carrying a 75-man raiding party nine miles up the shallow, twisting Sebou River to attack the important airfield at Port Lyautey. But standing in *Dallas's* way was a heavy wire-mesh boom, stretched across the river mouth under the muzzles of the Kasba's guns.

Lt. Comdr. Robert Brodie, skipper of *Dallas,* had been told that the barrier had been blasted open during the night by a demolition team. When he neared the barrier, though, Brodie was startled to see that it was only partly open. Splashes from the Kasba's shells were already wetting his decks. He wasn't sure the 22-year-old *Dallas* had the power to crash through the boom. And he knew that if *Dallas* got hung up on the barrier and became a stationary target, metal rather than water would soon be raining down on her. Nonetheless he ordered full speed ahead. *Dallas* hit the boom, shuddered briefly as her propellers churned up water as white as that thrown up by the shells falling around her—and then broke through.

Although he was free of the boom and soon out of range of the Kasba, Brodie's troubles were just beginning. The Sebou was so shallow that, during most of the passage, *Dallas* was slowed down by the soft mud of the river bottom, sucking at her keel. Occasionally machine-gun nests along the river's bank raked the destroyer's decks. Artillery farther inland took up when the Kasba's guns left off. But Brodie's gun crews were so expert— and so lucky—that they silenced every gun that was brought to bear on them almost as soon as it opened fire. *Dallas* in fact landed her raiders at Port Lyautey without having suffered a single casualty or a serious hit!

Once landed, her raiding party joined forces with an Army battalion that had marched overland, and captured the airfield by midmorning. And by noon P-40 fighters, flown in from escort

carrier *Chenango,* were berthed on the field, ready to join in
the all-out assault on Casablanca scheduled for the 11th.

Then out of the Mediterranean came surprising news. Shep-
herded by the British Navy, Anglo-American troops had met little
opposition at Oran and Algiers, and at Algiers had unexpectedly
found Adm. Jean Darlan, second to Marshall Pétain in the
Vichy government. Darlan, badly shaken by the impressive
strength of our landing force, had reluctantly agreed to discuss
a possible truce with a member of General Eisenhower's staff.
In the midst of the discussion, Darlan learned that the Germans
had reacted exactly as Pétain had feared; their troops had invaded unoccupied France. This news ended Darlan's reluctance
and, with Pétain's secret approval, on the night of 10 November
he sent a cease-fire order to all French forces in North Africa.
Thus, on the 11th there was no need to storm Casablanca. A
white flag flew over the city.

Two months later, in January 1943, President Roosevelt,
Prime Minister Churchill, and their Joint Chiefs of Staff met in
Casablanca to lay plans for the future. For the first time the
Allies' prospects were bright. Tojo was abandoning Guadalcanal
and MacArthur's Papuan offensive was rolling along. The Red
Army, taking advantage of the harsh Russian winter for which the
Germans were ill prepared, had launched a furious counterattack that threatened to break through the Nazi lines at several
points. In French North Africa the Allies were at last in a position to defeat the enemy's Afrika Korps. And once that was done
they could strike across the narrow Mediterranean at any number
of spots on the "soft underbelly" of Europe, as Churchill called it.

The major move agreed on at the meeting was Operation
Husky, an invasion of Sicily, the large island at the tip of the Italian "boot." From Sicily the Allies would then invade Italy, conquer that country and, at the same time, indirectly help Russia,
since the Italian army was so weak that Hitler would have to pull

some of his divisions from the Russian front and rush them to Mussolini's aid.

Operation *Husky* was scheduled for July, a date that for a time seemed too optimistic because defeating the Afrika Korps took longer than anticipated. In fact, the ground fighting in North Africa (which lies beyond the reach of this book) dragged on until the middle of May. Then 275,000 Axis soldiers were caught in a vise between the British 8th Army and the American II Corps and forced to surrender. It was the greatest victory yet won by Anglo-American arms.

It also allowed us to go ahead with Operation *Husky* on schedule, and on 9 July, 3,200 vessels, carrying an Anglo-American expeditionary force of 250,000 men, left Africa for Sicily. This immense fleet took Sicily's 300,000 German and Italian defenders so much by surprise that when the landings began in the dark morning hours of the 10th, no organized resistance was encountered. At dawn, though, the picture changed somewhat as the now-awakened enemy struck back with massed tank and air attacks. Even so, within a matter of hours the expeditionary force was able to seize 150 miles of the island's rugged coastline—and then the infantry struggle for Sicily began.

For the fleets involved, the job of escorting the expeditionary force safely ashore was relatively easy. The British Navy had long since sunk, damaged, or bottled up the Nazi's major warships. What was left of the Italian Navy didn't dare venture out of the harbor. And there were too few submarines and motor torpedo boats in the area to constitute a serious menace. Still, two naval aspects of *Husky* deserve mention.

For one, it was in this operation that the U.S. Navy's new and specially designed landing craft—which were to play an invaluable role in later amphibious operations—were first used. These were large LST's (Landing Ship, Tank), and small LCI's (Landing Craft, Infantry) and LCT's (Landing Craft, Tank).

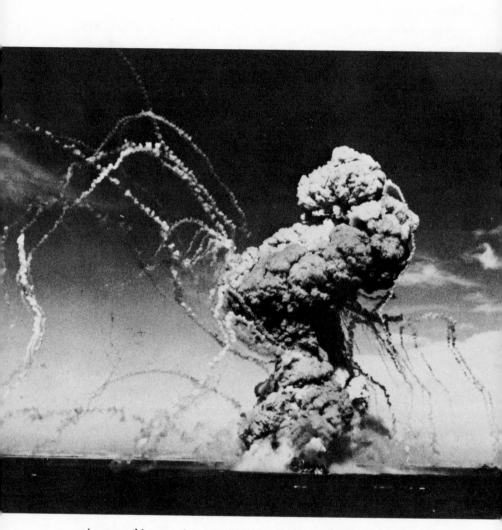

A cargo ship carrying munitions explodes after being hit by Nazi dive bombers during the Sicilian Invasion, July 1943.

They were shallow-draft, flat-bottomed vessels, with square bows that opened like doors, and ramps that lowered onto a beach. From them men, supplies, and all sorts of vehicles and artillery could be put ashore without having to be transferred to smaller boats. In addition there were the DUKW's, armored amphibious trucks which, like ducks, could move through water, clamber ashore, and then travel overland, carrying either soldiers or 2½ tons of equipment.

At Sicily, though, off some beaches there were sandbars on which many LST's, with their tanks and other assault weapons, got stuck. As fate would have it, too, at the beachhead where the enemy made his heaviest tank counterattack, an LST carrying all of the U.S. 1st Infantry Division's antitank guns got stuck and was blown up by German dive-bombers. So when enemy tank columns, including some mammoth 75-ton German Tiger tanks, lumbered onto the beach, our soldiers (unable to meet armor with armor) were pinned down in their foxholes.

Our cruisers and destroyers immediately moved in to give the 1st Division some desperately needed fire support. Throughout the day of the 10th, cruiser *Boise,* maneuvering so close inshore that her keel was barely clear of the sea bottom, dueled with and largely destroyed one column of 25 tanks. Another tank unit was turned back by destroyer *Shubrick.* On the following day, our warships were engaged with wave after wave of tanks and mobile artillery for 10 hours, their shells sometimes "splitting tanks open like a melon." And on the third day of this extraordinary land-sea duel, thanks to naval gunfire that reached farther and farther inshore, the 1st Division was able to widen its beachhead to a depth of eight miles.

As General Eisenhower said, at Sicily "naval guns were so devastating as to dispose finally of any doubts that they were suitable for shore bombardment."

After the third day Sicily's fate was sealed. The ease with which we'd landed and the speed with which we overcame their resistance so dismayed the enemy's high command that the Italians wanted to surrender at once. But the Germans insisted on fighting a delaying action, and fought it so well that Sicily didn't fall until 17 August—which gave the Nazis time to ferry most of their men back to the Italian mainland and in addition move several divisions from the Russian front to strengthen Italy's defenses.

In the meantime the Italian people, thoroughly sick of the war Mussolini had thrust on them, had in July forced the dictator to resign. He was replaced by Marshal Pietro Badoglio, who at once opened negotiations with the Allies and finally accepted their peace terms on 3 September. Yet when Italy's surrender was made public, the Allies were already mounting an amphibious assault on the Italian mainland, now destined to be defended solely—but stoutly—by Nazi troops.

Operation *Avalanche* was directed at the Gulf of Salerno, 30 miles south of Naples. Again it was a combined Anglo-American assault, and in view of Italy's surrender the men in the invasion armada were looking forward to an easy victory. Instead they got a bitter surprise. The Nazi's battle-hardened 16th Panzer Division was lying in wait for them.

The British soldiers, landing eight miles to the north of the beachhead assigned the U.S. 5th Army, suffered least. They went ashore in the morning darkness of 9 September as amphibious troops should—under the cover of a barrage showered on the Nazis' coastal defense positions by the guns of the Royal Navy. But the men of the 5th Army had no such protection. Their field commanders, ignoring Eisenhower's praise of naval shore bombardment, insisted on muzzling the guns of Admiral Hewitt's task force. A naval shelling of the beach, they said, would deprive their troops of the advantage of tactical surprise.

This was military wishful thinking at its worst; if for no other reason that landing craft motors are as noisy as anything afloat. Small wonder then that as the men of the 5th Army neared the beach, they were greeted in German-accented English by a voice calling through a loudspeaker, "Come on in and give up. We've got you covered." Dozens of flares followed the taunt, and in their glaring light the approaching landing craft were easy targets for German machine guns. So, tragically, many Americans died who might have lived had the Navy been allowed to soften up the beachhead.

In an unmatched display of bravery, the survivors fought their way ashore and dug in at the water's edge. Then for six days the opposing forces engaged in some of the war's fiercest fighting, with the Army now only too glad to accept naval fire support. And it can be argued that this support actually won the day. At least, after the Panzer Division retired and left Salerno to the Allies, on 15 September, the Nazi Commander in Chief in Italy, Field Marshal Kesselring, said that he'd ordered the retreat "in order to evade the effective shelling from warships."

Not until four months later were the American and British Navies again involved in the Italian campaign. Then after Kesselring and the 18 Nazi divisions he commanded had halted the Allies' northward march up the Italian "boot," the two navies were called in for another amphibious operation. This one—aimed at Anzio, 37 miles from Rome—was supposed to be an end run around the Germans' defensive position that would land our troops behind the enemy's line.

The landing was a success in the sense that our troops got ashore without too much trouble. But their commanders were too hesitant and Kesselring's countermoves were too swift to make the landing worthwhile. Kesselring's planes sank or damaged a number of transports and small warships. And his infantry moved in so fast that it pinned down the landing force before it could get rolling, and kept it pinned down all through the winter and spring months of 1944. So as one military expert says, "What should have been a spearhead became instead a beleaguered fort."

After Anzio there was no naval action in Italian waters. But for the Allied ground troops the Italian campaign was the longest and one of the most bitterly contested of the entire European war. A British general, Sir Henry Wilson, described it as a "slow, painful advance through difficult mountain terrain against a determined enemy, skilled in the exploitation of natural obstacles by mines and demolition." Marshall Kesselring's retreat northward was in fact so skillfully fought that it took the Allied Armies 600 days to force him to strike his flag in May 1945.

The battle for Italy cost the Allies 312,000 killed and wounded, the Germans 556,000. As for the Italians, among the comparatively few who died as a direct or indirect result of the invasion was one whose death was little mourned. For when it became clear that the campaign was going to end in an Axis defeat, Mussolini tried to flee his country. But he was found hiding in a farmhouse by an enraged mob of his own people and promptly executed. Then his body was hung by its heels in a public square for all to jeer at—bringing to a brutal and ignoble end an equally brutal and ignoble career.

And now it is time to look again to the Pacific, where the Navy, after breaching the Bismarck Barrier, began building a second road to Tokyo, using bombs and naval shells for paving blocks.

CHAPTER 7
✸✸✸✸✸✸✸✸✸✸✸✸✸

The Mitscher Shampoo

Memorial Day 1943 was an especially memorable day for a fleet that had grown weary of operating on a shoestring, for on that day the 25,000-ton *Essex* steamed into Pearl Harbor. She was the first of a new class of fast large carriers, the first of the many *Essex*-class carriers which in the days to come would join forces with the only veterans still afloat, *Saratoga* and *Enterprise*. Some of these new flattops would bear old familiar names: *Lexington, Hornet, Yorktown,* and *Wasp*. Others would have new names, like *Intrepid, Hancock, Franklin, Bunker Hill,* etc.

At this time, too, other newcomers were beginning to nose into the Pacific. With American shipyards now in full production, from mid-1943 on scarcely a week passed without a mammoth new 45,000-ton battleship, a brand-new cruiser, or a speedy new destroyer squadron dropping anchor in Pearl Harbor. More powerful in every way than their pre-Pearl Harbor counterparts, these newcomers could also do better than 30 knots, and had to to keep pace with the *Essex*-class carriers. Nor was this the only new carrier class being added to the fleet's air arm, for during this period of rapid build-up it also received several 10,000-ton *Independence*-class light carriers, built on the same slim fast hulls used for cruisers, as well as dozens of smaller escort carriers.

With the carriers came a badly needed new fighter plane, the F6F (Hellcat). When the war started, the Navy had been

Six Essex-*class carriers in Ulithi Anchorage, from foreground to background: USS* Wasp, *USS* Yorktown, *USS* Hornet, *USS* Hancock, *USS* Ticonderoga, *and USS* Lexington.

shocked by the discovery that its F4F (Wildcat) carrier fighters were inferior to the enemy's Zekes. The Zeke not only had twice the combat range of the F4F but could also outmaneuver and outclimb it. In its favor the F4F had two features the Zeke lacked: an armor-plated cockpit to protect its pilot and thick self-sealing fuel tanks that kept it from flaming as easily as a Zeke. Yet it was the added weight of the tanks and the armor-plate that accounted in part for the F4F's sluggish performance. So for every pilot these safety features saved, another was probably lost because they made his plane less maneuverable than that flown by his foe.

Once the F4F's weaknesses became known, the American aircraft industry went to work to build a better plane, and in carrying out its task performed one of the outstanding production feats of the war. It usually takes several years to design, test, and mass-produce a new plane, but the F6F, almost miraculously, was turned out in less than two!

By the Navy's impersonal statistics, in aerial combat the F6F outscored the Zeke 13 to 1. Less impersonal was the comment of a pilot who, after shooting down three Zekes, said, "That Hellcat is beautiful. If she could cook I'd marry her." As for the enemy's reaction, a noted Japanese ace said after the war, "The F6F (Hellcat) was speedier than the Zeke and could outclimb, outdive, outgun, and outperform it . . . In overcoming the Zeke's advantages you did much to hasten our defeat."

What did far more to hasten the enemy's defeat, though, was the fact that by August 1943 there were enough new planes and warships in the Pacific to form two independent fleets. The smaller one, Admiral Kinkaid's 7th Fleet, was organized solely to support amphibious landings, and assigned to General MacArthur to help him travel the road from New Guinea to the Philippines. The larger, Admiral Spruance's 5th Fleet, had an amphibious unit too—Rear Admiral Turner's 5th Amphibious

Force, nicknamed the "5th 'Phib'." But the 5th Fleet also had something new under the naval sun—the Fast Carrier Task Force, 5th Fleet, known as TF 58.

Commanded by the gnomelike veteran of Guadalcanal, Admiral Mitscher, at full strength TF 58 was made up of four fast carrier task groups. A task group in turn usually consisted of 4 carriers (3 *Essex-* and 1 *Independence*-class), 3 battleships and a like number of heavy cruisers, 4 attack and 4 antiaircraft light cruisers, and 20 or more destroyers. Each task group, then, was strong enough to operate alone, and sometimes did. Together, the four groups formed the most powerful armada ever employed in naval warfare, and gave enemy fliers an awesome bird's-eye view of 40 square miles of ocean dotted with 200 warships on the prowl.

Moreover, TF 58 was *always* on the prowl, always steaming into enemy-held waters on strikes of longer range than had ever before been known. Thus from the first moment it put to sea, TF 58 was able to keep the Japanese off-balance. They never knew where or when our fast carriers would catch them napping; never knew by what magic they were able to move so swiftly from one distant target to another.

Yet the magic was as simple as it was revolutionary. The ships of every other navy in the world, the Imperial Navy included, had to put into port every 2 or 3 weeks to refuel and replenish. The U.S. Navy on the other hand had perfected a complex technique for bringing tankers alongside warships and refueling them at sea while they were still making 12 knots speed. Besides, each fast-carrier task group was followed wherever it went by a Mobile Service Squadron of supply ships that it met at secret rendezvous at sea to take on everything from replacement planes and pilots to beans and bombs.

Unlike the Imperial Fleet, then, TF 58 could stay at sea, fighting without letup, for months on end. This unique staying power and mobility was known to the Navy as TF 58's "secret weapon"—and there is no question that it added immeasurably to the deadly efficiency with which the 5th Fleet sent the Japanese reeling as it opened up a long-awaited second front in the Pacific.

In any war, attacking simultaneously on two fronts confuses your enemy and forces him to split his forces, because he can never be certain of the direction from which your next major assault will come. For a two-pronged thrust to succeed, though, you must be able to man both fronts with at least adequate, if not superior, forces. And because of its Pearl Harbor losses and its later loss of four of its six carriers, Admiral Nimitz' original fleet had come perilously close to defeat while fighting on just one front. So much as he had wanted too, the admiral had had to postpone opening a second front until he had received enough reinforcements to form the 5th Fleet. Only then did he have the strength to begin building a second road to Tokyo by way of the enemy's Central Pacific flank.

The Central Pacific was chosen as a second front in part because it had advantages that other possible fronts lacked, in part out of necessity. It was necessary because the Gilbert, Marshall, Caroline, and Marianas Islands sprawled across the entire Central Pacific north of the equator, forming a network filled with hundreds of small fortified islands and atolls and dozens of larger ones with fleet anchorages and strategically placed airfields. And as long as Japan held these bases, she could by a dozen routes feed in air and naval forces to attack MacArthur's flank as he traveled the New Guinea-Manus-Philippines road to Tokyo.

Our Central Pacific strategy, then, was to a degree prompted by the need to protect MacArthur's flank. But more was involved. Every high-ranking American officer was convinced that Japan could only be defeated by invasion, and equally certain that no invasion could be successfully mounted until all of Japan's industrial cities, airfields, and military stockpiles had been destroyed by intensive aerial bombardment. So our first offensive goal in the Central Pacific was to penetrate deep enough into the enemy's defensive perimeter to place our land-based bombers within reach of Japan.

This was one of MacArthur's goals too. But once he recaptured the Philippines, in itself a formidable task, we would then be faced with the monumental problem of wresting Formosa and Hong Kong from the enemy, to gain the control of the South China Sea necessary to enable us to establish airfields on the Chinese coast. Equally monumental was the logistics problem this plan posed—the time-consuming length of a supply line running from the United States to Australia, then north to the Philippines.

By contrast, an island-hopping operation through the Gilbert, Marshall, Caroline, and Marianas Islands would lead us to Japan by a much shorter and more direct route. In fact, the largest of the Marianas Islands, Saipan, was only 1,300 miles from Tokyo —an easy hop for our immense new B29 (Superfortress) bombers.

The road to Saipan, however, was heavily barricaded by Japanese bases in the Gilberts and Marshalls. So when the 5th Fleet sortied for its baptismal amphibious operation, its chief target, logically, was Tarawa, the enemy's key position in the Gilberts and the gateway to the Marshall Islands farther north. Its secondary target was Makin, an atoll near Tarawa, which was to be taken for use later as an airfield. D-day was 20 November 1943.

There were more than 200 ships in the fleet, almost evenly divided between the 5th 'Phib Force, whose transports carried 25,000 troops, and TF 58. What is most noteworthy, though, is that when Spruance took TF 58 to sea he had with him more carriers than any admiral had ever before commanded—enough to put 900 planes in the air! This was an air fleet strong enough to neutralize the enemy's airfields in the Gilberts, fight off any

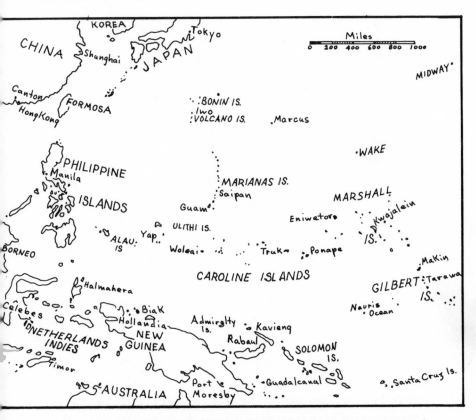

*While our forces invaded the Philippines to form one front, a second
front was opened in the central Pacific with an island "leapfrogging"
campaign through the Marshall and Marianas Islands to establish air-
bases for reduction of the defenses of the home islands of Japan.*

plane attacks from the Marshalls, and at the same time deal
with the Imperial Navy—or so Spruance believed.

True enough, the Gilberts' airfields were knocked out, and
all but one of the few dozen Marshall-based planes the Japanese
sent in were either shot down or turned back by F6F's. (One
torpedo plane got a hit on lightcarrier *Independence*, forcing
her to withdraw for repairs.) But Spruance's belief that TF 58
was strong enough to support an amphibious operation and at

the same time take on the Jap Navy was never put to the test. For when Tojo learned of the 5th Fleet's carrier strength, he ordered Japan's "Z" plan for employing her main naval forces in the defense of the Gilberts-Marshalls area canceled, thinking it wiser to hold the Combined Fleet in reserve for the protection of more crucial areas nearer his homeland. The cancellation was not extended, however, to nine submarines that were already at sea, bound for Makin and Tarawa.

The story of Makin is easily told because there the landing was easy and the ground fighting light. Unfortunately, though, the 6,500 infantrymen who overcame Makin's 800-man garrison took five days to do the job—an "infuriatingly slow advance," as their commander put it, for which the Navy paid heavily. It gave a submarine time to reach the scene and sink an escort carrier that was patiently providing air cover for the slow-moving ground troops. The carrier, *Liscome Bay,* lost 644 men, our infantry 64.

At Tarawa atoll the story was vastly different. There the enemy's strength was concentrated around his airfield on Betio, one of 26 islands encircling the atoll's lagoon. Betio was a mere 300-acre speck in the broad expanse of the Pacific, no larger than an average American farm and, like a farm, "fenced in" by a reef lying about 500 yards offshore. Yet tiny as it was, our aerial reconnaissance photographs indicated the island was fortified at perhaps a hundred points with artillery emplacements, antiaircraft and coast defense guns, and concrete blockhouses.

While this was a forbidding defensive network, no one in the 5th Fleet doubted for a moment that it could be knocked out by aerial bombardment and naval gunfire. Once that was done, it was taken for granted that Major Gen. Julian Smith's 2d Marine Division, 16,000 strong, would seize the island with ease. Confidence ran so high, in fact, that one naval briefing officer told his Marine audience, "Gentlemen, we don't intend to neutralize Betio. We will obliterate it."

The "obliteration" began at dawn on 18 November, when TF 58's pilots began pasting the island's ground installations. The pasting went for two days, 445 bombing missions were flown, and after the last one our bombers said "everything in sight" had been demolished. Then to make doubly sure that the island's destruction was complete, on the morning of D-day four battleships, five cruisers, and nine destroyers pounded away at Betio for three hours. By nine in the morning, after 3,000 tons of explosives had been poured on Betio's defenders, no one saw any reason to question a message from a scout plane that said, "Island looks devastated. Every square foot pockmarked with holes. No signs of life."

With this encouraging report in hand, the first assault waves were sent away—three Marine battalions in 93 "amphtracs" (armored amphibious tractors designed to crawl over coral reefs and then operate on land as tanks), followed by a wave of LCM's loaded with Sherman tanks and their crews. It was the Navy's first attack on a fortified atoll, its first attempt to send landing craft across a reef under fire, its first use of amphtracs as troop carriers—and the last time the Navy would ever launch such an assault with a false optimism born of its own miscalculations.

For Betio was far from obliterated, and the Marines were heading into a lethal trap. What went wrong? Many things. For one, the Navy had seriously underestimated the enemy's genius for fortifying his island bases. There were actually 500, not 100, separate fortified points on tiny Betio. But most of them were so low-lying and cleverly camouflaged that they showed up on reconnaissance photographs as nothing more than clumps of tropical vegetation.

Betio's beaches were lined with pillboxes and machine-gun nests, spaced 20 yards apart. Behind them lay a maze of artillery emplacements, tank traps, rifle pits, more pillboxes, and reinforced blockhouses cunningly connected by trenches and tunnels.

Many strongpoints were shielded by 7-to-12-foot-thick roofs of concrete, coral sand, and coconut logs. The island was pitted with enough bombproof shelters to protect its entire garrison. And the garrison itself consisted of 4,500 picked men, all but 17 of whom bravely lived up to their pledge to fight to the death!

Obviously, the Navy had grossly miscalculated the amount of bombing and shelling needed to soften-up Betio. There were tactical failures in close air support and communications too. Due to a lack both of practice and experience, throughout the operation carrier planes assigned to strafe or bomb an area a Marine unit was about to attack arrived on station either too late or too early. As for communications, they were faulty at both ends. The mobile radios carried ashore were too weak and fragile, and the radio system on General Smith's command ship, *Maryland,* was jarred into silence whenever the battleship fired a salvo.

Nor had enough thought been given to Betio's natural hazards, its reefs and the tides that washed them. This oversight in itself almost led to our defeat, because the first wave of Marines drew an unusually low tide. As a result, all of the LCMs got hung up on the reef and had to discharge their tanks into four feet of water, which drowned most of their engines. Of the 93 amphtracs, only two survived. Many conked out on the reef, the rest were sunk because they were too lightly armored to withstand the withering fire of the waiting Jap machine gunners.

The same withering fire was then directed at the Marines, left floundering as their amphtracs sank, who had to struggle 500 yards through neck-deep water that was soon stained with blood and dotted with bodies. With the enemy throwing everything he had at them, it's astounding that any of the waders reached the shore. Yet some 1,500 did, only to be pinned down on a narrow exposed beach by the enemy's ferocious crossfire, unable to advance, too heroic to retreat.

By early afternoon they were still pinned down, still suffering heavy casualties, and in such desperate straits that a call went out for a release of the division's reserve strength—a call that ended, ominously, with the phrase, "Issue in doubt." Then a slowly rising tide came to the Navy's aid, and by the end of D-day it had ferried a total of 5,000 Marines ashore and a beachhead had been established. It was a pitifully small one, though, only 300 yards long and 70 deep, and it was won at the highest price in American military history. Those few square yards of blood-drenched sand cost the Marines at least 1,500 casualties.

On the following day, with more favorable tides, fresh battalions fought their way ashore and the Marines began their victory push. It lasted 60 hours. In those hellish hours the Japanese fought with the fury of trapped animals, and the Marines attacked with a courage that was almost beyond belief. Time after time they charged blockhouses, pillboxes, and other entrenched positions with nothing but their hand weapons. Time and again men who had been hit kept going until a second or third wound brought them down, and then begged doctors to patch them up so they could return to their outfits. When they were told it couldn't be done, some cursed bitterly, some cried with frustration, and one dying captain asked a doctor to carry an apology to his men for "letting them down."

Men of such valor were not to be halted. By the night of 23 November Betio was in their hands, almost 4,500 Japanese were dead, and the first American plane had landed on the airstrip. By the 28th, seven less strongly defended islands had been seized. Then the atoll was ours, and the name Tarawa had become as much a legend in Marine history as the Halls of Montezuma and the Shores of Tripoli—a legend written, tragically, in the blood of more than 3,000 dead and wounded Leathernecks.

It was a terrible toll to pay, yet in one sense it was worth paying, because the mistakes made at Tarawa were never repeated. There we learned the techniques of the most complex forms of amphibious warfare the hard way. And because they *were* learned, for every life lost at Tarawa many others were saved in future landings.

We learned, for example, that our ship-to-shore-to-air radio networks had to be improved, both to eliminate the confusion that results when landing-force commanders afloat lose touch with their subordinates ashore, and to enable officers on shore to talk directly to their supporting warships and planes and pinpoint for them the exact ground targets they should zero in on. The number of escort carriers assigned to the 5th 'Phib' was increased, and their pilots were taught the most effective tactics for attacking shore installations. The gunners of the 5th 'Phib's battleships (those raised from the mud of Pearl Harbor, which were too slow to keep pace with TF 58) were trained for the first time to shoot at stationary shore targets, rather than moving ships.

In addition, more heavily armored amphtracs were rushed into production and armed with 75mm. cannon. Underwater Demolition Teams or UDT's were trained to blow up reefs and

A member of a Navy Underwater Demolition Team. These men, unarmed and unprotected, swam into enemy held beaches and braved enemy fire to blast invasion channels for U.S. amphibious landings.

other obstacles standing in the way of tank-carrying and other large landing craft. (Their frogmen were not, however, trained to put signs on beaches reading "Welcome U.S. Marines." That was their own idea.)

While the 5th Fleet's landing forces were being "remodeled," Admiral Mitscher's TF 58 was busily engaged in the Marshalls. Knowing these islands would be our next objective, the Japanese were steadily reinforcing them with more and more men and planes. They planned too and were confident they could fight a lengthy "holding" operation in the Marshalls, and thus gain the time they needed to make Saipan impregnable. But their confidence was soon shattered.

What shattered it was the thorough way in which TF 58 massaged the Marshalls with bombs. The massaging went on continuously from 29 January to 6 February 1944. It wrecked the entire air flotilla the enemy had assembled in the Marshalls. And it was the first but not the last time TF 58's planes gave the enemy the type of going over that later became famed as "The Mitscher Shampoo."

After TF 58 had cleansed the enemy's airfields of planes, Admiral Turner brought up his revamped 5th 'Phib' Force and seized the Marshalls with an ease that surprised him as much as it dismayed the Japanese. Incredibly, it took only three weeks.

The enemy's main base was Kwajalein Atoll, 10 of whose many small islands were fortified, three with Betio-like defenses. Yet Kwajalein fell in seven days, after its principal islands had been so softened up that they looked to one observer "like they'd been lifted 10 miles high, then dropped, kerplunk!" Admiral Turner then moved on to Eniwetok, leap-frogging four lesser bases and leaving them "to wither on the vine." Eniwetok is the northernmost atoll in the Marshalls and was strategically important because it lies only a thousand miles from the Marianas. It was subdued in six days. The cost of the two operations—almost un-

Gunners aboard the USS Yorktown *score a direct hit on a Japanese torpedo plane off Kwajalein.*

believable when you remember Betio—was 711 American casualties, as against 10,547 Japanese!

For good measure, while Eniwetok was being overrun, TF 58 was far to the west raiding Truk, the enemy's boasted "Gibraltar of the Pacific." Because Truk—the atoll in the Caroline Islands to which the Combined Fleet had retreated from Rabaul—was uncomfortably close to the Marshalls and closer yet to the Marianas, Admiral Nimitz had always assumed that the stronghold would have to be captured before we could move safely on to Saipan. So when he learned from intelligence reports that the Combined Fleet was still there, and that the atoll's airfields were jammed with planes, he ordered TF 58 in to the attack. It was as good a time as any to begin softening up Truk, and there was a chance too that the enemy's fleet would be caught napping.

But while TF 58 was en route to its target, the Japanese Fleet, realizing that time was running out for Truk, was withdrawing to new bases at Palau, 1,200 miles farther west, and Tawi Tawi near the southern Philippines. It was a move made out of necessity, not cowardice, since the Imperial Navy remained a force to be reckoned with. It now had 11 battleships, 40 cruisers, 90 destroyers, 9 carriers, and more warships abuilding. In the defense of Rabaul, though, it had lost so many pilots and planes as to leave its carriers seriously undermanned and almost useless. With new pilots being rushed through training and new planes being ferried to its carriers, the Combined Fleet for the moment was merely marking time. Once it was again at full strength, it would give a dramatic answer to the question our sailors were asking, "When's that damned Jap Navy going to come out and fight?"

Despite the escape of the enemy's main naval forces, TF 58's raid on Truk turned out to be one of the most important of the war. The atoll's airstrips held 365 land-based planes, and its lagoon held a couple of light cruisers, two destroyers, and a number of merchant ships. Pouncing on all of them with lightning swiftness, Mitscher's pilots quickly destroyed 200,000 tons of shipping, a cruiser, botn destroyers, and 275 planes. This alone would have made the raid worthwhile. But then all of Truk's harbor, supply, and repair facilities were given a Mitscher shampoo that reduced them to smoldering ruins. In their two-day attack, in fact, TF 58's pilots eliminated the need of invading Truk and spared us a costly amphibious operation. Thanks to them, the so-called Gibraltar of the Pacific was now just another enemy base that could be leapfrogged without fear.

Thus, in three short weeks in February 1944 the Marshalls fell, Truk was neutralized, and a deep wedge was driven into the outer crust of Japan's defenses. It was an amazing display both of the 5th Fleet's striking power and its growing mastery of amphibious warfare. But the crucial test of its capabilities was yet to come— in the Marianas.

CHAPTER 8

✢✢✢✢✢✢✢✢✢✢✢✢✢

The Great Turkey Shoot

Operation *Forager,* the occupation of the Marianas, was our boldest challenge yet to the enemy, because with the islands lying within easy bombing range of his homeland, he could be counted on to defend them with every weapon he could muster, including the Imperial Fleet. He simply could not afford to fight a holding operation in the Marianas as he had in the Gilberts and Marshalls.

The Japanese could also be trusted to take every advantage of the tactical situation, which favored them greatly. The Marianas were not low-lying coral atolls but large solid land masses with plains and plateaus and small mountains whose many caves were ready-made gun emplacements and bomb-shelters. Saipan, Tinian and Guam—the group's only islands of military importance—could in addition house larger garrisons than any coral island could hold. For example, on Saipan, 14 miles long by 5 miles wide, there were 29,400 troops, six times the number of Betio's determined defenders, as well as the enemy's largest aviation installation in the Central Pacific, Aslito Field. In fact, it was because of Aslito Field that we struck Saipan first. The airfield had to be neutralized to prevent its planes from harassing our later landings on Tinian and Guam.

The logistics situation was also against us, since our nearest supply and staging base, Pearl Harbor, was 3,500 miles from Saipan. Never before had the Navy had to convoy such a large number of troops—three Marine and two Army divisions, totaling 127,571 men—such a great distance, then hold open a supply line of that length. And with many more assault troops assigned to *Forager* than in any previous operation, a much longer preinvasion training and rehearsal program was needed, of course.

To give the 5th 'Phib Force time to prepare for such a complex undertaking, it was in fact necessary to delay D-day until 15 June, almost four months after the fall of Eniwetok. This posed another problem. For the Japanese knew that we would eventually strike the Marianas. And if we let four months pass without keeping up the pressure on them on both fronts, the chances were that they would feel free to shift most of their reserve strength to the Marianas. So, during those months, Nimitz and MacArthur conspired to confuse Japan's warlords and keep them from concentrating their uncommitted reserves around Saipan.

For his part, MacArthur speeded up his timetable for mopping up New Guinea and took Hollandia in April, two months ahead of schedule. Hollandia was a major Japanese airbase on the northwest coast of New Guinea, and sandwiched between the base and the general's front lines lay Wewak, the encampment of the only significant enemy force left in New Guinea, the 18th Imperial Army. Thus, in seizing Hollandia in a smoothly executed amphibious hop, MacArthur not only bypassed but trapped an entire army.

Then on 27 May the general leapfrogged from Hollandia to Biak, a large island to the north of New Guinea. With Rabaul neutralized and Manus in American hands, Biak was the most important roadblock still standing between MacArthur and the Philippines, and his landing on the island left the enemy no choice. The Imperial High Command had to make every effort to hold Biak and had to send reinforcements to the island that might otherwise have been used in the Central Pacific.

In the same months TF 58 was rampaging through the Central

Pacific, raiding a dozen widely separated islands and doing all it could to trick the enemy into keeping its reserves spread thin. In April, for instance, Mitscher's carriers hit Palau with such violence that the Japs hurriedly sent out a call for reinforcements to be rushed in from as far away as Singapore to oppose what they thought was the start of a major offensive in the Western Carolines. As another example, in May TF 58 steamed to within a thousand miles of Tokyo to bomb Marcus Island. In response to this daring raid the Imperial High Command issued a new order calling for planes in outlying bases to assemble in Japan proper "to annihilate any enemy fleet which approaches for an attack close to our homeland."

When TF 58 finished its mission of deception it retired to the Marshalls, where Admiral Spruance was assembling the largest armada the Navy had yet readied for action. In Mitscher's task force there were 15 carriers, 7 battleships, 21 cruisers, and 69 destroyers. In addition, to convoy its 250-odd transports and auxiliary vessels and then provide close-in air and fire support for the landing troops, the 5th 'Phib Force now had 14 escort carriers, 5 battleships, 12 cruisers, and 122 destroyers and de- stroyer escorts. All told, when Spruance took the 5th Fleet to sea on 6 June he had under his command 535 ships, not counting the dozen or so submarines already stationed in the sea lanes leading to the Marianas to scout the movements of the enemy fleet.

Once under way, TF 58 left the slower 5th 'Phib Force and sped ahead to the point in the Philippine Sea 200 miles off the west coast of Saipan from which it was scheduled to strike the first blow of *Forager* on 11 June. And a crushing blow it was. Instead of doing what had always been done before— launching a dawn attack in hopes of catching the enemy napping —Mitscher shrewdly waited until late afternoon to send off a fighter sweep of 225 F6F's. It was an absurdly simple change of tactics. Yet it caught the Japanese off guard, with so many of their planes grounded at Aslito and other airfields that 147 of them—one-third of the enemy's entire air strength in the Marianas—were sitting ducks for our fighters, who for their part lost only 11 planes.

While the strike didn't eliminate all airborne opposition, it reduced it so sharply that it gave TF 58 almost complete control of the air over the Marianas. With this won, the 5th Fleet could then safely proceed to soften up Saipan as planned.

On the 12th and 13th, Mitscher's fliers bombed and strafed airfields, troop concentrations, and whatever gun emplacements they could pinpoint. On the 13th, too, TF 58's battleships moved in to lash out at Saipan with their 16-inchers. On the 14th, the fury of the bombardment was increased when the 5th 'Phib Force reached the scene and sent its planes and warships in to maul the island too. The 14th was also the day the UDT's charted the existing channels in the offshore reefs and blasted new ones where needed.

But since Saipan was 160 times larger than Betio it was impossible to blanket all of the island's 81 square miles with explosives, much less pulverize the defense installations the enemy had emplaced in caves and hewn out of solid rock. It was hoped though that the Navy's supporting fire could keep the 29,000-man garrison pinned down long enough to enable our troops to get ashore with minimum losses. To this end, at dawn on the 15th, D-day, the brunt of the bombardment was shifted to the four-mile stretch of beaches where the landings were to be made. First they were given a three-hour pounding by a column of battleships, cruisers, and destroyers steaming less than a mile offshore. Then as the initial wave of 150 troop-filled amphtracs churned shoreward, the naval fire was lifted inland to make way for a low-level sweep of the beaches by 160 bombers and 72 planes armed with rockets.

Yet concentrated as the bombardment was, many of the enemy's skillfully camouflaged mortar and machine-gun positions

The battleship USS Missouri fires her 16-inch guns. Six projectiles can be seen in flight in the upper right of the photograph.

Carrier planes staged attacks to keep the Japanese defenses spread thin while troops moved up the central Pacific. Much of the Japanese power in the Caroline Islands was left to "wither on the vine," kept in isolation by our sea power.

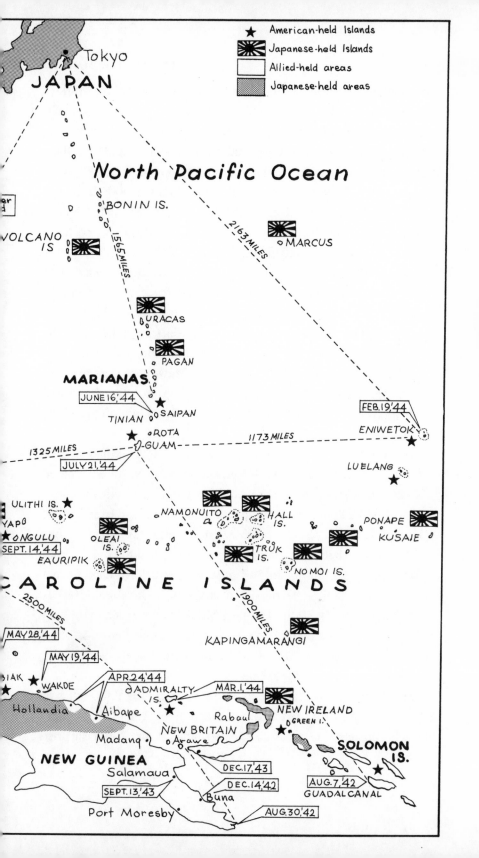

escaped destruction. Consequently, the first wave of Marines encountered heavy fire as it hit the beaches. Nonetheless, in 20 minutes 8,000 Marines were ashore, grimly inching their way toward the entrenched Japs, and by nightfall 20,000 Leathernecks held a beachhead that in places extended 1,500 yards inland. It was ground that cost the Marines 2,000 dead and wounded. But it was a firm beachhead. And in the next two days 57,000 more men were funneled through it and thrust into three weeks of bloody ground fighting that ended as disastrously for Japan as the naval action which was about to be joined. For as had been anticipated, an enemy carrier force, Adm. Jisaburo Ozawa's 1st Mobile Fleet, was speeding to Saipan's defense.

There were nine carriers in the enemy fleet, as opposed to the 15 in TF 58, and fewer screening warships too. Moreover, few of the pilots manning the 430 planes on Ozawa's carriers had had more than six months' training. Mitscher on the other hand had 956 aircraft, 475 of them F6F's, and almost all of his pilots were combat veterans.

Although Ozawa was aware that he was badly outmatched he was still confident of victory, for he knew that in warfare a tactical advantage is frequently more important than numerical superiority. And he held a considerable tactical advantage over TF 58. His lightly built planes, lacking armor plate and heavy self-sealing tanks, had a far greater range than Mitscher's. His scout planes could search out to 560 miles and still have enough fuel left to return to their carriers, Mitscher's no more than 350. His attack planes had a 300-mile range, Mitcher's not much more than 225. So as Ozawa pictured the upcoming engagement, his scout planes would locate TF 58 while his own force was still too distant to be spotted by Mitcher's search planes. And once he'd found TF 58, he would close to within no more than 300 miles of it and, with his own carriers out of reach of an American counter-attack and hopefully still undetected, launch an all-out surprise attack.

But TF 58 was not to be taken by surprise. In fact, Spruance had learned that Ozawa was at sea on D-day, when two U.S. submarines reported an enemy carrier force in the westernmost reaches of the Philippine Sea. Calculating that it would take the Japanese four days to cross the sea, Spruance planned accordingly. He ordered the unloading of troops and supplies to continue through the 17th, after which all noncombatant vessels were to scurry east of Saipan to safety. He ordered the 5th 'Phib Force's warships to stand their ground and continue supporting the troops on Saipan, but postponed the landing on Guam scheduled for the 18th.

Instead, on the 18th Spruance led TF 58 to a position 160 miles west of Saipan, set up a battle line on a north-south bearing, then ordered Mitscher's planes to search for Ozawa to the outer limit of their range. It was as far from Saipan as Spruance dared to go. His first duty was to our invasion forces, and he could not risk steaming so far west than an "end run" by an enemy he still hadn't located, might expose our troops on Saipan to a mauling by Ozawa's guns and bombers. Nor had the situation changed by nightfall, since none of the searches Mitscher sent out was successful. So during the long night of the 18th all TF 58 could do was wait and hope that Ozawa's course would bring him within range of a dawn search.

It didn't, though, because on the 18th Ozawa's scout planes had found TF 58, and thereafter he had skillfully maneuvered to escape detection. Thus, at daybreak on the 19th he was still some 380 miles to the west; too far to be spotted, yet near enough to steam east at full speed and be in a position to launch his first strike at 8 o'clock in the morning.

The chapter of the Battle of the Philippine Sea that all Navy men remember as "The Great Marianas Turkey Shoot" opened at 9:59, when our radars picked up the incoming raid 150 miles to the westward. Within five minutes every ship in the 5th Fleet's fighting arm was at general quarters. On Mitscher's carriers tense voices were shouting through loudspeakers, "Now hear this! Fighter pilots man your planes!" And on *Enterprise,* as pilots sprinted across the flightdeck, chartboards in hand and oxygen masks flopping from their helmets, a voice added, "Now we're going to give the Japs their half of the Pacific—the bottom half!"

It was a prophetic remark. For as Admiral Spruance said later of the conflict that was shaping up, "There was nothing else like it in the whole of World War II." It was the greatest naval air action in history. Four times as many planes were involved as at Midway. They dueled continuously for eight hours. Yet in truth it was less a battle than a massacre. It was such a slaughter, in fact, that for once statistics best tell the story.

Starkly stated, at dawn on the 19th Ozawa had 430 planes, at nightfall only a hundred—and 76 of these were planes he had held back to fly combat air patrol over his fleet! Because of the confusion of the eight-hour melee no one knows the exact box score. Certainly most of the enemy planes sent to their half of the Pacific were shot down by our F6F's, an unknown number fell victim to antiaircraft fire, and some damaged planes undoubtedly crashed while trying to return to their carriers. But this we do know. Only 30 American planes were lost in the day's dogfighting. What is equally incredible, of the more than 350 attacking Jap planes only one got a hit, with a 500-pound bomb that the battleship *South Dakota* took in stride.

Nor was all of the shooting done in the air. On the morning of the 19th the submarine *Albacore* slipped through Ozawa's destroyer screen and with a single torpedo exploded the aviation gas storage tanks of Japan's newest and largest carrier, the 33,000-ton *Taiho,* sending her to the bottom of the Pacific with most of her crew. Three hours later a veteran of the Pearl Harbor strike, the carrier *Shokaku,* met the same fate when three torpedoes from *Cavalla* tore open her hull.

Since Ozawa's losses on the 19th were so staggering that he no longer posed a threat to Operation *Forager,* Spruance was

An aerial view of the Japanese fleet under attack by carrier-based U.S. aircraft west of the Marianas, 19 June 1944.

This photograph, taken aboard the USS Kitkum Bay, *shows a Japanese plane crashing in flames during the Saipan Operations.*

free to send Mitscher in pursuit of him. It began as a blind pursuit, because, during the Turkey Shoot, our planes had been too busy to search for the enemy fleet. And it continued blind until almost 4 o'clock on the afternoon of the 20th, when a scout plane from *Enterprise* finally spotted the 1st Mobile Fleet, fleeing at 24 knots, about 275 miles to the northwest of TF 58.

Because time was fast running out, Admiral Mitscher had to make a quick and agonizing decision. Sunset was at 7 o'clock. It would be 4:30 before he could get a strike airborne. To attack Ozawa and return, his pilots would have to fly a minimum of two hours out, two back, and fight in between. The problem was as obvious as it was grave. As Mitscher said later:

> Taking advantage of this opportunity would cost us a great deal in planes and pilots, because we would be launching at the maximum range of our aircraft and at such a time that it would be necessary to recover them after dark. This meant that all carriers would be recovering daylight-trained air groups at night, with consequent loss of some pilots, none of whom were familiar with night landings and all of whom would be fatigued at the end of an extremely hazardous and long mission.

But for two days Ozawa had remained maddeningly out of reach and was even now almost certain to escape entirely unless this opportunity was seized. So Mitscher really had no choice but to order, "Man aircraft!" Nor is there any doubt that the scrappy little admiral meant it when he added longingly, "Give 'em hell, boys; wish I were with you."

At 4:20 the turn into the wind to launch aircraft began, and in a record-setting 10 minutes 216 planes from 10 carriers were airborne. They sighted the enemy at 6:40—from a sky whose cloud cover and setting sliver of a new moon foretold a black night ahead—and struck at once. With their nearly half-empty fuel tanks they had no time to organize coordinated attacks. It was every man for himself.

Pushing over from 15,000 feet, Mitscher's boys plummeted

down through the heaviest antiaircraft fire they had yet encountered; straining their eyes, looking at the same time for
targets in the fading light below the deadly fireworks and Zekes
in the cloudy sky above. Dive-bombers released missiles on ships
they could scarcely identify. Torpedo planes groped through
the dusk for the familiar silhouettes of carriers. F6F's swept in
low, strafing any deck caught in the cross-hairs of their gunsights.

The attack lasted until the sun sank and darkness blotted out
the scene, for which Ozawa could only have been thankful. For
in roughly 20 minutes Mitscher's air groups sank two tankers
and the heavy carrier *Hiyo,* badly damaged *Zuikako,* and lightly
damaged two smaller carriers, three cruisers, and a battleship.
The action cost Ozawa 56 out of his 100 surviving planes,
forcing him to end his log entry for 20 June with the line.
"Surviving carrier air power: 35 operational planes." And on
the morning of the 19th he had had 430!

American losses in the twilight action were 20 planes. Thus
196 were still aloft in the black sky, still at least 275 miles from
TF 58. And after flying for an hour or so on their homing leg,
after their full-throttle dives and after the ack-ack and the Zekes,
they were all nearly out of fuel above a dark and empty ocean.
Then in desperation many pilots broke radio silence and the air
began to fill with alarming messages: *Can anyone tell me where
I am? . . . Can you read my position? I'm outta gas and have
to ditch. . . . Gotta spare pickup destroyer? My gauge reads
less than empty . . . Give me the course back. Repeat. Please
give me a course.*

A few planes began to go down. Most managed to continue
eastward though, and at about 8:45 the homing signals of the
American carriers, 35 miles away, began to beep faintly in their
pilots' earphones. Comdr. Edward P. Stafford, who was aboard
Enterprise that night, has described what happened next in his
book *The Big E:*

The carriers called the planes down, but only a few lucky or exceptionally skillful ones were getting aboard. The sky overhead filled up. Engines coughed, cut out . . . and minutes later splashes tore the sea around the force.

The biggest disaster in aviation history was in the making. The pilots needed lights. But there was a war on. Enemy snoopers were in the air. Enemy subs had to be around. There were perhaps 350 men in the 200 aircraft circling overhead and inbound. One torpedo spread could sink a carrier with 2,500 men aboard. Logic demanded that the ships stay darkened and the airmen land as best they could. Destroyers could pick up survivors in the morning.

Aboard *Lexington,* wrinkled Pete Mitscher slipped down from his chair on the bridge, where he had been watching and listening, and walked through the blackout curtains into Air Plot, blinking at the sudden light. He perched on the arm of a brown leather couch, lit a cigarette, and said four words, "Turn on the lights."

TF 58 sprang out of the darkness as though a master switch had illuminated a World's Fair. Thirty-six-inch and twenty-four-inch searchlights poked bright fingers into the sky. Red truck lights glowed on all mastheads. The carriers turned on their deck-edge lights, and destroyers fired star shells, lighting up the sea for a mile in all directions.

Mitscher could not let his pilots down. He took a chance that no Japanese, Russian, Chinese, or German admiral would ever have thought of taking. . . . Seldom have four words made a man so beloved by so many.

Because of Mitscher's courageous and humane gesture 116 planes landed safely, although, in the hurry, half of them landed on the wrong carriers. The remaining 80 planes ran out of fuel and had to ditch, but alert destroyers managed to rescue most of their crews, floating in their rubber life rafts. As a result, all but 16 pilots and 33 crewmen of the 401 airmen who had flown that day's reckless mission were recovered.

For the full two days of the Battle of the Philippine Sea our losses were 130 planes, 76 airmen. The enemy lost three of his large carriers, 395 carrier planes, and what was far worse, almost that number of carrier pilots. This was the third time Japan's air groups had been all but wiped out. Consequently, Ozawa's six surviving carriers, with their empty flight decks, were practically useless. In other words, Japanese carrier aviation was virtually finished as a naval force in the war.

Inevitably, too, Ozawa's defeat sealed the fate of the Marianas. With the 5th Fleet in complete command of the waters and air surrounding the islands, the enemy's garrisons on Saipan, Guam, and Tinian were totally cut off from outside help. So it was just a question of time until they were annihilated by our foot soldiers, backed up by continuous naval fire support.

Bombardment of Guam by 14-inch guns, July 1944.

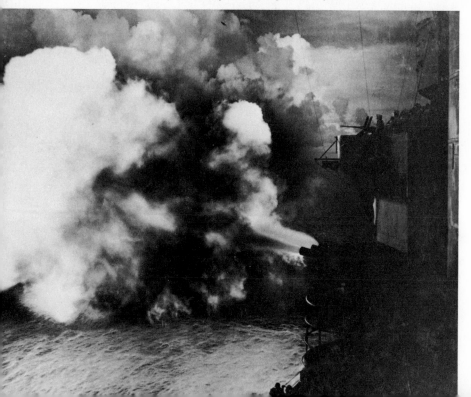

The USS Pennsylvania *bombarding Guam preparatory to invasion,*
20 July 1944.

Helldivers returning from strike on Guam, July 1944.

Saipan fell on 9 July, Tinian on 1 August, and Guam on 11 August, exactly two months to the day after the opening shot of Operation *Forager*. But the story of the Marianas does not end with their conquest, for it was there that the Navy's Construction Battalions performed their outstanding feat of the war.

Nicknamed the Seabees, these Construction Battalions did the war's dirty work. They moved hills, bridged rivers, made roads, built harbors, paved airstrips in the jungles, built anything anywhere it was needed—and in their spare time frequently fought the enemy. They were, in one admiral's words, "The unsung heroes of the steam shovel and monkey wrench; brave men who built victory by sweat."

In the Marianas the Seabees' most important assignment was to build airfields capable of handling our huge new B29 Fortress

Seabees at work in the Pacific.

bombers, which, with their long range, could fly with ease from the Marianas to both the Philippines and the Japanese home islands. To say simply that the Seabees carried out their assignment in short order is an understatement. On Tinian, for example, they built what was then the world's largest airport—six bomber strips a mile and a half long and a block wide, connected by 11 miles of taxiways leading to enough "hardstands" to park 300 bombers—and completed the job in 73 days! On Saipan and Guam, too, they built similar though smaller airfields with equal speed. Thus it was the Seabees who were largely responsible for the fact that bombs began falling on Tokyo while the enemy was still reeling from the loss of the Marianas.

It seems clear too that most members of the Japanese government suspected that Japan's chances of winning the war had vanished with the fall of the Marianas, because on the day the Japanese people were told that Saipan had been overrun, Tojo and his cabinet were forced to resign. The ruthless warlord was replaced as premier by Gen. Kujaiki Kosio, who was charged with giving "fundamental reconsideration" to the problem of continuing the war. But after reconsidering, the Imperial High Command still could not bring itself to admit defeat. Instead, it steeled its fighting force to another year of desperate resistance, in the false hope that the American people might yet tire of bloodshed and negotiate a peace from which Japan could still salvage some spoils of war.

There was, it seems, only one high-ranking Japanese officer who had the courage to face the facts. He was Adm. Osami Nagano, the Emperor's naval adviser who, when told of the loss of Saipan, summed up the future of Japan for Hirohito with the blunt words, "Now all hell is on us!"

His words could just as well have summed up what was then happening on the other side of the globe, where for Hitler's Germany all hell was breaking loose, too.

CHAPTER 9

✿✿✿✿✿✿✿✿✿✿✿✿✿

Bows Against the Beach

On 6 June 1944—the same day the 5th Fleet weighed anchor for Operation *Forager*—in England the Supreme Headquarters, Allied Expeditionary Forces announced:

UNDER THE COMMAND OF GENERAL EISENHOWER, ALLIED NAVAL FORCES, SUPPORTED BY STRONG AIR FORCES, BEGAN LANDING ALLIED ARMIES THIS MORNING ON THE NORTHERN COAST OF FRANCE.

This was the momentous day an enslaved continent had eagerly awaited. It was D-day for Operation *Overlord,* the sledgehammer blow the Allies had been planning for two years and the crucial move in the Beat-the-Axis-First strategy, as Eisenhower's message to his troops that day made clear:

Soldiers, sailors and airmen of the Allied Expeditionary Force: You are about to embark on a great crusade . . . In company with our brave Allies and brothers in arms on other fronts you will bring about the destruction of the German war machine, elimination of Nazi tyranny over the oppressed peoples of Europe, and security for ourselves in a free world . . .

The tide has turned . . . I have full confidence in your courage, devotion to duty and skill in battle. We will accept nothing less than full victory. Good luck, and let us beseech the blessing of Almighty God upon this great and noble undertaking.

For Germany the tide was clearly ebbing. Hitler's U-boats had lost the Battle of the Atlantic. Allied bombers had been rain-

151

ing explosives on German cities and key war production centers for months. In Italy, where after a winter of bloody stalemate Allied armies had broken Field Marshal Kesselring's defensive line, 18 Nazi divisions were in jeopardy. After staving off what seemed certain defeat on the eastern front, Russia had mustered 330 divisions to pit against Germany's 172. And in May 1944 the Red Armies, after killing or capturing a million Nazi soldiers, had gone on the offensive along a 1,400-mile front.

Yet the ebbing tide still had a distance to go. Germany's war machine had only been weakened, not crippled. And nowhere was it stronger than along the steel and concrete studded French coast of the English Channel. There 58 Nazi divisions lurked behind what Adm. Alan Kirk, the chief American naval officer in *Overlord*, called "the most formidable barrier ever known to fighting man."

For almost four years at least a half million of German's political and military captives, brutally driven by Nazi guards, had been fortifying the rocky cliffs and pebbly beaches of France's northern coast. These slave laborers had been forced to salt the coastline with an estimated million land mines, pour concrete for countless pillboxes and heavy gun emplacements, dig antitank traps, clear passages for mobile artillery, string barbed wire, and plant underwater obstacles and mines. Everything possible had been done to make this long fringe of beach assault-proof, and Hitler was so confident of its strength that he openly boasted that his Atlantic wall was "impregnable."

Although Allied war planners didn't believe his boast, neither did they scorn it. They were fully and uneasily aware that in attempting to breach the wall they were undertaking one of the most complex and hazard-ridden operations in military history. So they prepared for *Overlord* with a thoroughness which is a story in itself.

The operation was so carefully planned that a full set of its naval orders alone weighed 300 pounds. Equally bulky orders, thought through to the last second and last inch, were drawn up for the ground, air, and logistics forces. And as for the weight of the forces themselves, it was jokingly said at the time that the British Isles would have sunk into the sea had they not been supported by barrage balloons.

The joke was born of the presence in the Isles in the spring of 1944 of 2.8 million soldiers, sailors, and airmen; more than half American, the rest Canadian and British. There were in addition 11,000 aircraft, wingtip to wingtip on dozens of airfields. The countryside was dotted with hundreds of fields jam-packed with tanks, trucks, amphtracs, jeeps, bulldozers, and guns of every caliber, under camouflage netting. Massive ammunition, fuel, and supply dumps filled innumerable pastures. And in most of the Isles' bays and harbors there were fleets of transports or squadrons of the 4,000 landing craft and 700 U.S. and Royal Navy warships assigned to the operation.

Nor was that all. In the battle a single army division would need about 600 tons of supplies a day, and the Allies planned to put 37 divisions ashore in the first weeks of the onslaught. To support them the Allies had to have both safe anchorages for their supply ships and docks on which to unload their cargoes. But the beaches to be stormed were lacking in harbors and fully exposed to the pounding seas for which the English Channel is infamous. So some British ports were also filled with "Mulberries"—huge concrete caissons which were to be towed across the Channel and sunk offshore to form two artificial harbors, complete with docks, for the all-important supply ships.

There was also enough flexible four-inch pipe piled up in England to lay 20 pipelines across the bottom of the Channel, through which a million gallons of gasoline a day could be pumped. Finally, to replace the bomb-shattered French railroads the Allies had ready an entire railway system, complete with flatcars, rails, and locomotives.

With such a vast gathering of men and materials there was,

of course, no way of concealing from the Nazis what was coming. However, since only a select few of the highest Allied commanders knew exactly *where* and *when* the blow would come, no enemy espionage agent was ever able to learn what the Germans most wanted to know—which of the many French beaches were to be the target of *Overlord*. As a result, the Allies' elaborate "Deception Plan" worked to perfection.

To pin down large numbers of German troops far from the chosen battleground, a phantom invasion army was "assembled" on the English coast at the Channel's narrowest point, opposite the Pas-de-Calais region of France. Fleets of dummy landing craft were marshaled in the Thames River estuary, dummy tanks were placed where they could be seen from the air, and many large but empty tent encampments were erected in nearby fields. At the same time a radio and wireless network was set up to imitate the heavy communications traffic of a major force preparing for an attack.

Then fictitious information about the plans of a so-called "1st Army Group" was leaked in such a way that it fell into the hands of known enemy agents. As a final touch, the air bombardment preceding the actual invasion was craftily designed to create the impression that the Pas-de-Calais region was being softened up more thoroughly than other sections of the French coastline.

The masquerade worked even better than anyone had hoped. For the Germans not only concentrated their strongest single force in France—the 15th Army, 19 divisions strong—on the wrong coast. They also found the masquerade so convincing that for more than two weeks after the invasion began they thought *Overlord* was nothing more than a large-scale feint, and that the major blow was yet to come on the Calais coast. So the German high command kept the 15th Army standing idly by in Pas-de-Calais at the very time it was most needed some 150 miles away to the southwest, in Normandy.

Overlord's real target was a group of beaches about half-way up the Cotentin Peninsula on the Normandy coast. There two American and three British divisions were to be landed simultaneously; the British on beaches with the code names "Sword," "Juno" and "Gold"; the Americans on beaches "Omaha" and "Utah."

Prior to D-day, the Allied Air Forces had been flying round-the-clock missions for three months, pounding most of the western fringe of Europe. They had paralyzed the coastal radar network designed to warn the Nazis of the approach of a hostile fleet. To hamper German troop movements our bombers had not only made a "railway desert" of northern France but shattered most of the region's bridges too. And our fighter pilots had reduced the strength of the already weakened *Luftwaffe* to the point where Eisenhower could confidently tell his men, "Don't worry about planes. Any you see will be ours."

The loading of assault troops started on 1 June. After being briefed on their mission the men were "sealed" in their transports, to prevent any from going ashore and indulging in loose talk. Then the great invasion armada waited tensely for the final "this is it" message.

D-day had originally been set for 5 June but bad weather forced a 24-hour postponement. So the armada didn't nose into the still wave-heaped Channel until the night of the 5th, when our air attacks rose to a last-minute pitch of fury and 18,000 seasoned paratroopers jumped behind the German lines to harass the enemy from the rear. Then for the next 24 hours the fate of Europe lay in the hands of the British and American Navies, or, more specifically, in the amphibious fighting skill of the Eastern Naval Task Force, Adm. Sir Philip Vian, RN, commanding, and the Western Naval Task Force commanded by Adm. Alan Kirk, USN.

In describing the historic crossing Admiral Kirk said, "It was a masterpiece of farsighted planning. A fleet of 4,000 ships, converging from half of the points of the compass, and of varying sizes and speeds, reached the rendezvous with split-second timing. And from that time on, all those vessels continued to operate with the same split-second timing.

"Minesweepers were already far ahead, sweeping channels right into the beaches and dropping lighted buoys to mark the swept channels. Guidance vessels were posted to direct traffic into the proper lanes at every turn in the courses. Inside the 1,000-yard line were other vessels to guide the assault boats in the final dash to shore.

"All across the Channel the great armada stretched, with battleships, cruisers, and destroyers guarding the van and flanks, and an umbrella of air coverage giving protection against air attack . . . Then the bombardment ships moved in and began hurling an avalanche of shells against the surprised Nazi pillboxes, entrenchments, and gun emplacements. The old battleship *Texas* opened fire at 12,000 yards; the old *Arkansas* moved in to 6,000 yards—a bare three miles. The destroyers delivered their fire at such close range that, as one observer put it, 'They had their bows against the beach.' That avalanche of shells beat down German heavy 88's and 105's high up on the bluffs above Omaha Beach; it hammered the concrete gun emplacements amid the dunes and swampland of Utah Beach.

"Then the troop carriers, reaching the Transport Area, lowered their assault craft. The troops swarmed into them, and the amphibious craft chugged shoreward to challenge the Nazis' 'impregnable' wall with their loads. Already, ahead of them, demolition teams were driving in through the shallow water, blowing up underwater obstacles under a hail of enemy bullets. Too, heavy enemy mobile guns began to open up with a heavy crossfire, and casualties were heavy. Offshore vessels were struck, to flame up or lie helpless and sinking. Now especially trained U.S. Coast Guard craft plunged into the heavy fire, making heroic rescues as they pulled men from the water or from flaming wrecks. Then, in the end, ships' gun fire searched out the hidden guns and put them permanently out of commission."

So much for the general picture. As might be expected, though, the close-in fighting varied on different beaches. In the British sector, Gold, Juno and Sword Beaches all had barrier reefs which were exposed at low water, blocking the route to the shore. So there the landings were held up for two hours to give a flood tide time to rise. Because of the unexpected delay, the Royal Navy had two hours of full daylight—as compared to the half hour of daylight the U.S. Navy had—in which to bombard shore installations before the first assault wave touched down.

Owing to this two-hour pounding of the beach defenses with high-caliber shells and the presence in the area of only a single German division, the landings at Gold, Juno, and Sword were comparatively easy. So easy, in fact, that by nightfall the three divisions put ashore (two English and one Canadian) were linked up on a broad front five miles inland. Thereafter, though, the nature of the fighting changed quickly, as Nazi motorized divisions rushed to the scene and bitterly contested every inch of ground the British and Canadians gained in the following month.

On the American flank, the unexpected again played an important role at Utah Beach. There the U.S. 7th Corps' first wave, touching down precisely at H-hour (6:30 a.m.), waded ashore with scarcely a shot being fired at it. If this was surprising, the landscape the invaders faced was even more so. It had none of the terrain features shown on their maps, bore no resemblance whatever to the beach they had been trained to attack. In their 10-mile boat trip ashore, head winds and a strong southerly current had driven them off course and set them down a mile below the beach they were supposed to hit.

It was a lucky mishap. They had headed for a strongly defended beach with concrete-encased guns that might well have slaughtered them, as they later learned, and landed instead on

an almost defenseless beach. Fortunately, too, they were led by
Brig. Gen. Theodore Roosevelt, Jr., the only officer of flag rank
at Normandy whose request to go ashore with the first wave—
"to steady my boys"—was granted. Realizing at once what had
happened, Roosevelt quickly adjusted his tactics to the unexpected terrain confronting him, then radioed instructions for following waves of landing craft to make for the "wrong" beach
too. By nightfall, as a result of the mishap, at Utah it had cost the
Corps only 197 casualties to put ashore more than 21,000 men
and 1,700 armored vehicles, and liberate more than 36 square
miles of French soil!

Omaha Beach was a different story. It was guarded by three
times more men than Allied Intelligence had estimated, including
a crack German division that had just moved into the area to
practice anti-invasion tactics. Moreover, the Nazis had taken
every advantage of the natural terrain of this stretch of beach,
which was ideally suited for defense.

Three rows of steel-and-concrete underwater obstacles blocked
the approaches to the beach. The beach itself, a 300-yard-wide
strip of sand, was booby-trapped, and also exposed to the crossfire of eight heavy guns in bunkers and 120 machine- and antitank guns. Above the beach a seawall, partly made of boulders
and partly of poured cement and log pilings, was both mined
and strung with barbed wire. Behind this barrier lay a level
grassy area some 200 yards deep, again heavily mined. Landward
of this level shelf was a line of cliffs, topped by gun emplacements
and too steep for tanks or other tracked vehicles to climb. The
only possible exits from the beach were four deep ravines cutting
into the cliffs, through each of which ran a dirt track that was
covered for its entire length by the muzzles of the heavy guns
emplaced in the sides of each of the ravines.

As one admiral put it, Omaha Beach was "the best imitation
of hell" any American soldiers would encounter in Europe. To
make matters worse, the Navy wasn't given enough time to do

much damage during its pre-invasion bombardment, because it was feared that additional bombardment time would give the enemy additional time to bring up reinforcements. Nor were matters improved when our warships lifted their fire to clear the air for 484 heavy bombers of the 8th Army Air Force. The bombers were supposed to demolish whatever strong points survived the Navy's brief shelling—but they missed their mark so badly that their bombs fell three miles inland!

Small wonder then that the men of Gen. L. T. Gerow's 5th Corps who hit Omaha Beach at H-hour were the unluckiest in all of Operation *Overlord*. As naval Lt. W. L. Wade of Landing Craft Group 28, said, "Enemy fire was terrific—105mm, 88mm, 40mm, mortars, machine guns, everything. And very few shells fell to seaward. They waited until our landing crafts lowered their ramps, then cut loose with everything they had. Rocketboats and gunboats didn't faze them in the least . . . A lot of our men who did get ashore were sprawled out on the beach like a human carpet, subject to everything the Germans could throw . . . It seems a miracle this beach was ever taken."

The first casualties of that bloody morning were not foot soldiers, however. They were the heroic men of the 16 UDT's sent in to blast channels through the underwater beach obstacles with the 40-pound charges of TNT each man carried. Working in shallow water and in full view of the enemy, they were under constant fire. One 12-man team was wiped out by a mortar barrage. Another lost every man but one when, by chance, a shell struck a TNT packet. Other teams suffered lesser losses. But the survivors stuck to their job and blew five channels through the close-packed obstacles.

Then from a mile offshore LCT's launched the amphibious tanks which were supposed to clear the beach of machine-gun nests before the first wave of infantry landed. The tanks were equipped with canvas waterwings, nicknamed "bloomers," to keep them riding high in the water during their shoreward voyage.

But the "bloomers failed to bloom," and in the rough seas kicked up by the previous day's storm, 27 of the 32 tanks assigned to the eastern flank of the beach sank, taking their crews with them. Seeing this tragedy from afar, the commander of the LCT's on the western flank ordered his craft to brave the enemy's fire and drive their bows onto the beach before unloading, which they did—only to have most of their 32 tanks immediately shot up by German artillery.

So when the first LCI's dropped their ramps there was no armor on hand to aid the infantrymen who charged into the pounding surf. Not that it mattered to the GI's whose craft took direct hits as they were beaching or those who were killed by fusilades before they reached dry land or even to those who made the beach and were then blown to bits by mines or felled by the enemy's withering crossfire. (One company lost two-thirds of its men and all of its officers in the first few minutes, another 35 of 70 men in the first hour.) But for those who survived the loss of the tanks was critical, because their hand weapons were no match for the enemy's heavy stuff. To add to their predicament, the men had lost leadership, too, since most of their officers were dead or wounded. So the survivors could only lie hunched on the sand or huddled under the seawall, wondering what to do next.

The story was repeated when the second infantry wave landed at 7 o'clock, repeated again when the third wave rolled in. Nor was help forthcoming from the artillery units scheduled to begin landing at 8 o'clock. The field pieces were loaded on DUKW's amphibious trucks that could carry a 2½-ton load ordinarily. But the choppy seas off Omaha Beach were too much for the DUKW's, all but five of them drowned, and consequently only a single Army battery managed to reach shore.

Thus by 9 o'clock a disaster seemed in the making. Our troops had been ashore for 2½ hours and were still pinned down at the water's edge along the entire stretch of beach—with no relief in sight. Things looked so dark, in truth, that on their command ship General Gerow and his immediate superior Gen. Omar Bradley were seriously considering evacuating their men and shifting them to Utah Beach.

Then Rear Adm. Carlton Bryant, commanding the Omaha Beach Support Group, took a hand. Having sized up the situation from the bridge of his flagship *Texas,* at 9:50 he broadcast to his force, "Get on them, men! Get on them! They're raising hell with the men on the beach and we can't have any more of that. We must stop it!"

With this, Bryant's destroyers recklessly took over the role of the drowned artillery. All seven of them—*Frankford, Doyle, Harding, Thompson, Baldwin, Emmons,* and *McCook*—charged into water so shoal they sometimes scraped bottom, seldom had more than a few inches of water between keel and sand. They were so close against the beach their spotters could see targets with the naked eye and no longer needed binoculars, so close that in shooting it out with German batteries dug into the cliffs they had to point their 5-inchers almost skyward. *McCook* was the first to get a "Well done!" from Admiral Bryant, for knocking out three pillboxes and six emplaced guns. By nightfall, though, every destroyer in the squadron had won the admiral's praise.

Farther out at sea, *Texas, Arkansas,* and three cruisers blasted away with equally telling effect. One cruiser silenced a heavy coastal battery with five successive direct hits—almost unbelievable marksmanship. Between them, *Texas* and *Arkansas* lobbed 771 rounds of 14-inch shells on the gradually crumbling German fortifications. During the morning they both trained their guns on targets of opportunity. By afternoon though there were fewer such targets and *Texas* was free to concentrate her fire on a single ravine, to help clear the exit from the beach toward which our troops were then moving.

Conditions on Omaha Beach had in fact begun to improve

as early as 11 o'clock, when the paint on the smoking naval guns was just starting to blister. By that time the enemy's fire had lessened so significantly that company leaders could begin moving their men forward, smoking out entrenched Germans as they went. Beginning then, too, fresh waves of infantry and artillery, and bulldozers and other equipment as well, could be ferried ashore with reasonable safety. Thus by late afternoon the first tanks began rumbling through the breached ravine. And by nightfall the beachhead, now a mile deep, not only held 34,000 men but was considered secure enough for General Gerow to set up his headquarters on land.

Once ashore, Gerow's first message to General Bradley was, "Thank God for the United States Navy." Later, one of Gerow's divisional commanders added, "Without naval gunfire we positively could not have crossed the beaches."

The praise was probably deserved. Yet no Navy man who was at Omaha can ever forget that the actual *crossing* of the beaches was done by U.S. infantrymen. They were the ones who suffered 2,000 casualties on D-day. They were the ones who fought their way forward when a wounded colonel called out, "Come on! They're murdering us here, so we might as well go inland to get murdered." They were the ones, too, who in the days that followed drove back the savage Nazi counterattacks, ordered by Hitler to "throw the invaders into the sea."

So in a single day the Allies broke the so-called "impregnable" wall. And within a week they were actually building up their invasion army faster than the Germans could reinforce theirs. For in that first week the temporary Mulberry harbors, assembled on D-day plus one, enabled them to bring in some 326,000 men, 54,000 vehicles, and 104,000 tons of supplies, and solidly consolidate a beachhead more than 7 miles long and from 5 to 15 miles deep. In the pet phrase of an English field marshal, everything was going "absolutely tickety-boo."

Then came a serious setback. The worst storm to strike the

English Channel in 40 years roared in out of the northeast, destroying one Mulberry, damaging the second, and wrecking or damaging 415 vessels besides. It was bitter proof that until the Allies took Cherbourg, a major French port on the tip of the Cotentin Peninsula, the Channel's notoriously foul weather would threaten their grip on Normandy.

Knowing they would need a permanent port to handle their shipping, the Allies had planned from the outset to take Cherbourg, but at a later date when their hold was firmer and their forces stronger on Normandy. Now capturing the port had to be given top priority, and on 22 June they went all-out for the city, both by land and by sea and with full knowledge of how formidable a fortress they were attacking. For the Germans, knowing too that the Allies would need the port to supply their armies, had garrisoned the city with 40,000 men and every type of weapon, including 11-inch coastal guns with a 20-mile range.

By land, the 7th Corps assaulted Cherbourg, spearheaded by three divisions that suffered 16,300 casualties in some of the war's bitterest ground fighting. At sea, *Texas, Nevada,* and *Arkansas,* and a mixture of British and American cruisers and destroyers fought it out with the foe's thundering coastal batteries. And just as at Casablanca, the centuries-old military axiom that naval ships cannot engage on equal terms with strong coast defense guns in permanent fortifications was proved false. With pinpoint accuracy our naval gunners pounded the enemy's harbor forts to a defenseless rubble. In return, only *Texas* and two destroyers were hit—none badly.

Cherbourg surrendered on 27 June, and its fall was vital to the ultimate success of Operation *Overlord.* Nor is there any question that the valiant 7th Corps played the major role in capturing the port. Even so, the Nazi commanders at Cherbourg cited "a naval bombardment of unequaled fierceness" as one of the chief reasons for their surrender. On this gratifying note, the last major engagement in the Atlantic theater of war in which

U.S. combat ships participated came to an end.

The ferrying of Allied troops across the Channel was now speeded up. (Appropriately, the millionth American landed on Omaha Beach on the Fourth of July.) On 24 July the Allies broke through the enemy's defensive positions in Normandy and fanned out in all directions, to begin the battle for the liberation of all France.

Then on 15 August came Operation *Dragoon,* a series of amphibious landings along the French Mediterranean coast. Ten divisions were put ashore by a task force commanded by Adm. Kent Hewitt, USN, forcing the Nazis to abandon their lightly held positions in southern France with undignified speed. As the Navy's official historian of World War II, Samuel Eliot Morison, says, "*Dragoon* may stand as an example of an almost perfect amphibious operation . . . But it met no opposition comparable to that encountered in Normandy. Moreover, *Dragoon* was launched two weeks after the big breakthrough, on a flood tide of victory. Its greatest accomplishment was to swell that tide by an entire Army group, which made the Allied advance into Germany irresistible."

Dragoon was our last naval operation in the Mediterranean theater of war. But the Navy's work was still not quite finished, for in the final stages of the European conflict it was called upon to perform one of the oddest jobs in its entire history.

After the Allies had fought their way through France and crossed the German frontier, Hitler ordered his armies to make a desperate last stand on the east bank of the Rhine River. It was a move that General Eisenhower had foreseen. And since crossing the Rhine would in its way be an amphibious operation—and a hazardous one at that, because the Nazis could be trusted to defend their Fatherland with a fanaticism born of despair—the general asked the Navy to help him make the crossing.

The request led to the formation of the almost unknown

"Rhine Fleet." It consisted solely of landing craft and Navy men
specially trained to deal with the navigational hazards peculiar
to rivers; swift currents and eddies, floating debris, and the
freshwater problems of mudbanks and silt. Since the fleet trained
mostly on the rivers of France and Belgium, when the time came
for it to assemble on the Rhine's west bank its landing craft had
to be carried overland to their destination by truck. "They arrived," one naval officer said, "festooned with treetops, telephone
wires, and bits of buildings from the French villages through
which they had passed like not-too-silent ghosts in the night."

For the sailors of the Rhine Fleet the trip overland was as
weird as it was unnatural, but once they reached the great river
they were back in their element. Old amphibious hands all, in
March 1945 they ferried five U.S. armies across the treacherous
waterway, with field artillery instead of the guns of warships
providing their fire support. Working round the clock was as
commonplace as zigzagging through a German artillery barrage.
Less commonplace was an occasion when the crossing was in
jeopardy. Then in the short span of 72 hours they scurried
across the shell-splattered river with more than 50,000 troops
and thousands of tanks, trucks, and badly needed pieces of
ordnance.

The Rhine Fleet was a curious one, and the only one in the
war to operate hundreds of miles from the sea. Yet it was more
than a curiosity, and it clearly deserves much more credit than
it has been given for the invaluable if minor role it played in the
final overwhelming assault on the Nazis.

The full story of the final drive into Germany belongs to the
valorous Allied ground troops. It is enough to say that they
closed in on Hitler so relentlessly that the once-arrogant dictator
finally cracked up. With his mad dream of conquest turned into
a nightmare of defeat, on the night of April 28 he shot himself
and joined the pitiful 30 million who had fallen victim to his
insane ambitions. The European war didn't end officially,

though, until an unconditional surrender document was signed by Germany's surviving leaders. Then the Joint Chiefs of Staff received the following telegram:

The mission of this Allied Force was fulfilled at 3 a.m., local time, 7 May 1945.

Eisenhower.

CHAPTER 10

✠✠✠✠✠✠✠✠✠✠✠✠✠

"Take Her Down!"

General Tojo said at the end of the war that one of the three main causes of Japan's defeat was the relentless sinking of her shipping by U.S. submarines, the other two being our leapfrog strategy and our fast carrier operations. This is why the Submarine Force, Pacific Fleet, more conveniently called Subpac, merits special mention. And now is the logical time to honor our submariners, because to understand some of the enemy's tactics in the battles that followed the fall of the Marianas it is first necessary to understand that he was to a large extent forced to adopt them because of the damage done his entire war machine by our undersea raiders' blunt-nosed torpedoes.

The old saying that combat ships are only as good as the men who sail them probably best explains Subpac's extraordinary war record, for no branch of the Navy was ever better manned than its submarine service. For one thing, every sailor in Subpac had volunteered for the extrahazardous duty of serving aboard an SS (naval shorthand for a submarine). And every SS skipper had been hand-picked for his intelligence, initiative, and hardihood. That they were all brave men too goes without saying. The timid don't go off voluntarily on missions deep into enemy waters, nosing through minefields and dodging depth charges, knowing full well that a submariner's chance of losing his life is six times greater than that of a sailor on a surface ship.

In the submarine service acts of unusual bravery were in fact

167

This photograph, taken through the periscope of the American sub-marine Wahu, *shows a Japanese destroyer that had just been hit by two torpedos launched by* Wahu.

so numerous as to be almost commonplace. Yet two of them must be singled out as examples of heroic self-sacrifice unsurpassed in any war. First, early in 1943 SS *Growler,* on station between Truk and Palau, surfaced on a foggy night to repair a hull rupture caused earlier in the day by depth charges from two Jap destroyers. But just as Comdr. Howard Gilmore and six of his men reached *Growler*'s open bridge, an enemy gunboat came charging in out of the fog, all guns firing. Two men were killed instantly. Gilmore, wounded and clinging to a railing ordered, "Clear the bridge!" Not realizing he was too badly wounded to move, his companions scrambled down the conning tower.

Below the entire crew then waited anxiously for Gilmore, knowing *Growler* would be sunk if she didn't submerge at once. Alone on the bullet-riddled bridge, Gilmore knew this too. So raising his voice above the roar of the sea and the guns, he shouted, "Take her down!" His men hesitated. With a gale of gunfire sweeping *Growler*'s superstructure it would be suicide to try and rescue their skipper. But he was still alive and conscious . . . Still they hesitated. Then they heard Gilmore's voice again: "I said take her down. That's an order!" So being disciplined fighting men they took her down—knowing their drowning skipper was sacrificing himself so that they and *Growler* could live to fight again.

West of the Gilberts a few months later, SS *Sculpin* engaged a Jap convoy. Aboard *Sculpin* in addition to her senior officer, Comdr. Fred Connaway, was Capt. John Cromwell, a high-ranking Subpac officer who knew many of the Navy's secret war plans. While closing the convoy at periscope depth, *Sculpin* was detected by the destroyer *Yamagumo* and so severely pummeled by 18 depth charges that she was in immediate danger of sinking. Taking the only course left to him, Connaway ordered, "Blow all ballast," then told his crew to prepare to fight it out on the surface with *Sculpin*'s deck guns.

It was no match. The SS had one 4-inch and two 20mm.

machine guns; the destroyer, six 5-inchers. *Sculpin* took a lethal hit at the waterline. Another smashed the conning tower, killing Connaway and three brother officers. There was nothing left to do but abandon ship. Scrambling topside in their life jackets, 42 men jumped into the sea and were later rescued by *Yamagumo*. But Captain Cromwell was not one of them. Not trusting his ability to stand up to the agonies of Japanese torture, he told *Sculpin*'s senior surviving officer, "Sorry, I can't go with you. I know too much." Then he went below to await *Sculpin*'s last dive.

Submarine Force, Pacific Fleet was fortunate too in having developed before the war a workhorse submarine as rugged and reliable as its fighting men. This *Gato*-class SS, as it was called was 312 feet long, displaced about 1,500 tons, and was manned by a crew of 7 officers and 70 men. It had a 10,000-mile cruising range, carried enough supplies to stay at sea 60 days, and had a surface speed of 20 knots. Submerged and running on batteries rather than its four diesel engines, it could pursue for an hour at 11 knots or creep off at 2½ knots for 48 hours, before having to surface to recharge its batteries. It, of course, had sonar "ears," and for "eyes" it had its periscope and both air- and sea-search radars. Finally, it had torpedo tubes aft as well as forward and stowage for 24 torpedoes.

There was a marked difference between the way we used our fleet submarines and the way the Japanese employed their I-boats, submarines which were as large as ours and carried more powerful torpedoes. Their strategy called for their I-boats to concentrate on sinking our warships, which they did with some success in 1942, as we have seen. Thereafter, though, as our antisubmarine tactics improved, they seldom got in a good shot. Then, too, they began to waste their submarines on foolish missions. They were sent off as far as the coast of Oregon to conduct meaningless bombardments. Equipped with watertight deck hangars and scout planes, many of them cruised for weeks to make reconnaissance flights of no real value.

Even more foolish was the Japanese Army's use of them. Early in the war its generals discovered that submarines could carry supplies and, as time passed, pulled more and more of them out of combat to furnish bypassed garrisons at Guadalcanal and other islands with rice and ammunition. As a result, by late 1943 we, in turn, were able to pull many of our destroyers out of convoy duty and use them instead in combat.

It's true that Subpac often sent boats on special missions, too, but never foolish ones. Nor did our submarines ever pass up a chance to sink an enemy combat vessel. But American strategy differed from Japanese in that it called for Subpac to devote its major efforts to the destruction of the foe's merchant marine rather than his warships, for a sound reason.

Japan was vulnerable. Her home islands were woefully poor in natural resources. The raw materials she needed to keep her factories running and her war machine operating had to be brought in by ship from the far-flung empire she had conquered in the first months of the war. Thus the Asiatic shipping lanes leading to Japan from her sources of oil, tin, rubber, and iron were like arteries feeding a heart. Cut them, sink Japanese shipping faster than it could be replaced, and in time the heart would stop beating. Destroy her shipping and Japan would be nothing but four beleaguered islands without an empire.

This is why the heaviest concentration of American submarines was always to be found off the mouths of Japan's major harbors, in the China Seas, and in the channels in the East Indies favored by enemy convoys. It was there that the hunting was richest; there that fat-bellied tankers, transports heavy with soldiers and guns, and supply ships deep-laden with raw materials were most often found.

Concentrating our torpedo-fire on the foe's merchant marine was sound strategy. Yet for almost 2 years it worked less well than it should have—for the surprising reason that for all of its boasted technological skills, in the beginning the United States provided its submariners with torpedoes that were inexcusably bad. It wasn't just that they carried a less powerful warhead than the enemy's. Nor was it the fact that an I-boat's torpedoes had a range of 11 miles and a speed of 50 knots, while ours did well to travel 8 miles at 26 knots.

What was worse was that all too many of ours were duds. During the first 18 months of the war, dozens of SS returned from war patrols and filed reports of torpedoes that had struck enemy hulls without exploding. But Washington's armchair admirals were hard to convince. They refused to believe the torpedoes were defective and suggested instead that Subpac's crews were inexperienced men who in time would steady down and begin firing their missiles properly. It wasn't an argument that sat well with Adm. Charles Lockwood, who for most of the war was Commander Subpac, and his sarcastic answer was, "Design us a boathook then, so we can rip the enemy's hull plates apart by hand."

The duel of words didn't end until July 1943, when SS *Tinosa* caught one of Japan's two largest tankers off Truk and pumped 11 torpedoes into the 19,000-ton vessel, yet failed to sink her because eight were duds! This was conclusive proof that we were manufacturing defective torpedoes, and tests were made which should have been conducted earlier—tests which revealed that time after time a contact exploder in a warhead failed to detonate because its firing pin was too fragile to stand up to the impact of a good square hit. It was an easily corrected defect and by September Subpac finally had a stock of reliable torpedoes—its first in 22 months of war!

After that there was no stopping our submariners. By mid-1944 they had in fact so badly crippled Japan's merchant marine that Subpac decided it could now afford to make an organized drive on enemy combat vessels too. And here again our undersea fleet showed its mettle, for as an official Navy publication says:

Armed at last with good torpedoes, in 1944 Subpac smote the Imperial Navy a stupendous blow. In this year American submarines sank 55 Japanese warships. The obituary embraced: 1 battleship, 4 carriers, 3 escort carriers, 2 heavy and 8 light cruisers, 30 destroyers, and 7 submarines. In addition they permanently disabled 3 heavy cruisers and 1 carrier.

The box score for the entire war shows that U.S. submarines accounted for nearly a third (201 of 686) of the warships Japan lost in the conflict—including one whose loss was unique by any standard. The memorable loss occurred only 150 miles off the mouth of Tokyo Bay and was inflicted by Comdr. Joseph Enright's *Archerfish*. On 28 November 1944 *Archerfish* made a surface contact with what appeared even at extreme range to be an unusually large carrier, with four destroyers in escort. The carrier's speed was 20 knots; too fast for *Archerfish* to make a submerged approach, so fast there was a question whether the SS could long keep pace with the carrier on the surface.

Fearful of losing his prey, Enright sent out a contact report, hoping to guide some submarines nearby into an intercepting position. The report was picked up in Pearl Harbor and Admiral Lockwood immediately sent Enright a dispatch; one that was typical only of the submarine service, which was so closely knit that enlisted men and officers alike seldom bothered with the formalities of rank. Lockwood's message was, "Keep after her, Joe. Your picture is on the piano."

Joe kept after her for seven hours, overloading his diesels to the danger point, yet slowly falling behind. Then came the break. The carrier veered sharply, placing herself almost on a collision course with *Archerfish*. Now Enright had his target right where he wanted it. Taking *Archerfish* down to periscope depth, he waited until the range closed to a mere 1,400 yards, then fired a salvo of six torpedoes, spread to smash into the enormous carrier from stem to stern. Enright saw the first two hit and a great glowing ball of fire flare up before he ordered "Take her down," then heard the other four explode before the destroyers began showering depth charges on him.

Enright knew that he had finished off a monster of a carrier. Not until after the war though did he learn that *Archerfish* had sent to the bottom not only the largest warship ever sunk by a submarine but also the youngest! His victim was the supercarrier *Shinano,* a 59,000-ton giant that had taken four years to build. Yet *Archerfish* had sunk her on the 17th day following her launching and within 24 hours of the time she weighed anchor for her first cruise—thus making *Shinano* the shortest-lived warship on record.

Despite the pummeling our submariners gave the Imperial Fleet, what unquestionably hurt Japan the most was the surgical efficiency with which Subpac severed the arteries feeding her industrial heartland. For as one authoritative analysis of the war says, "The strategic campaign against the Japanese merchant marine pursued relentlessly for 3½ years by U.S. submarines . . . steadily weakened Japan's industrial and fighting strength . . . Shrinking stockpiles of raw materials markedly reduced Japanese war production. An increasing shortage of bunker oil and aviation gasoline limited the operations of the Japanese Navy and Air Forces and forced them to such drastic measures as . . . the suicidal tactics they employed in the final battles of the war . . . [The campaign] greatly hastened Japan's final collapse."

Statistically, of the 2,117 merchant ships Japan lost, 1,150 were sunk by submarines, the others by aircraft, mines, and surface ships. Put another way, out of 10-million tons of non-combatant shipping sent to sea by the enemy during the war, less than 2-million tons survived—and a full 60 percent of the tonnage sunk was credited to submarines. This impressive score was run up by a fleet of 288 subs, only 48 of which were lost in combat, as against 130 I-boats destroyed out of 181. Even so,

3,505 U.S. submariners died in the line of duty, or six for every one nonsubmariner the Navy lost, excluding aviators. These casualty figures, however, are only arithmetical proof that the men of Subpac lived dangerously. For more dramatic proof, consider the risks the crew of the SS *Tang* took during what has been called "the most successful patrol ever made by a U.S. submarine."

With her veteran commander, Richard O'Kane, on the bridge, *Tang* left Pearl Harbor for her fifth war patrol in September 1944. Her destination was the Formosa Strait, a congested highway for enemy ships moving between the East and South China Seas. After cautiously inching through the thickly seeded minefield at the strait's nothern mouth, on 11 October, *Tang* sank two freighters. Then her luck ran out and she spent 12 days without even sighting a target.

On the night of 23 October her radar finally picked up a large convoy, Manila-bound under heavy escort. With such rich pickings in sight, O'Kane chose to risk a surface rather than submerged attack, and daringly headed for the heart of the formation. Slipping through the convoy's screen, he maneuvered *Tang* until she was literally surrounded by shipping, before unleashing the torpedoes in his bow tubes. They all sped true, each finding and mangling a ship's hull.

Then began a wild free-for-all. With the sea dotted with ships either blowing up or burning, the escorts knifed through the flame-lit night, firing everything they had at *Tang* as they closed in to ram her. Throwing her rudder now hard right, now hard left, *Tang* twisted and squirmed, at one time slipping between the bows of two converging destroyers just seconds before they collided astern of her, putting themselves out of action. Then a troop transport loomed out of the battle smoke, also intent on ramming the sub. Emergency speed and hard left rudder took *Tang* out of her path, only to leave the sub boxed in, with burning ships ahead, the transport and a tanker astern, and destroyers closing in from all sides. Ignoring the destroyers, O'Kane ordered, "Stand by for a shoot" and calmly emptied his stern torpedo tubes into the transport and the tanker.

Though his torpedo tubes were now empty, O'Kane next aimed his bow at the nearest destroyer and ordered full speed ahead. His bluff worked. Fearing a torpedo, the destroyer veered away sharply, opening an escape path through which *Tang* sped unscathed into quiet water and hastily submerged. While his men relaxed from their busy night's work, O'Kane noted in his log that during the encounter *Tang* had torpedoed seven ships, to bring her total for the cruise to nine.

Exactly 24 hours later, *Tang* picked up a second large convoy heading south to reinforce the Philippines. From his bridge O'Kane could see tankers, and troop transports whose open decks were piled high with crated planes. Deciding again on a stealthy surface approach, O'Kane closed the range to 1,000 yards before opening fire, both fore and aft, with six torpedoes; two aimed at one transport, two at another, and two at a tanker. All six drove home, four filling the night sky with flying debris, two spilling burning gasoline over the sea.

But again *Tang* was boxed in by a transport and tanker astern and a destroyer rushing in from one side and two destroyer escorts from the other. And again O'Kane turned on his attackers. But this time he wasn't bluffing. With the three torpedoes left in his bow tubes he stopped the destroyer dead in the water, brought the transport to a shuddering halt, and turned the tanker into a flaming geyser. It was shooting that was as quick as it was incredibly accurate, and it opened the gap he had to have to escape from the oncoming destroyer escorts.

Now *Tang* had only two torpedoes left to load, and at a safe distance O'Kane slowed down to check them. Since both seemed to be in order, he decided to return to the fray to polish off a crippled troopship. The first ran true and brought *Tang*'s record for the cruise to 15 ships torpedoed. But the second broached, made a hairpin turn, and reversed course. On *Tang*'s bridge a lookout screamed, "Circular run! Circular run!"—the most dreaded words in a submariner's vocabulary. At the same moment O'Kane ordered, "Right full rudder—ahead emergency!" It was too late, though. Within seconds the erratic torpedo slammed into *Tang*'s stern.

The blast blew O'Kane and eight of his men into the sea. *Tang,* mortally wounded, hesitated just long enough to allow some sailors the time needed to close the conning tower hatch, then plunged 180 feet to the bottom. All but 30 of her crew were dead, dying, or injured, her after torpedo room was afire, and although her hull, miraculously, had not been holed, elsewhere aft seawater gurgled through a dozen leaks. Yet there was no panic, no giving up in despair. Nor did any of her able-bodied crewmen make a move toward the escape hatches. Rather they turned to, to try and save *Tang*. Some fought fires, others leaks. The medical corpsmen did what they could for the injured and dying. Others showed their mettle and their discipline when they began burning *Tang*'s code books and secret papers, knowing full well that the smoke from the burning documents coupled with that from the fires might in the end suffocate them all. And they continued their burning even though a depth charge pounded *Tang*'s bow and started a second fire in the forward battery compartment.

The fight to save *Tang* went on for four choking, searing hours. By then, with leaks still leaking and even the paint on the bulkheads blistering, it was plain that *Tang* was doomed. By then, too, only 13 men were still on their feet and able to reach the escape hatch in the forward torpedo room. Of the 13 who could crawl into the escape trunk, though, only eight reached the surface through 180 feet of water. And only five of them were able to swim until morning, when, along with O'Kane and three of his companions, they were picked up by a gunboat, to begin their journey to a Japanese prison camp.

When they were recovered at the end of the war, Commander O'Kane was awarded the Congressional Medal of Honor. Part of his citation said:

> For conspicuous gallantry and intrepidity in combat, at the risk of his life above and beyond the call of duty . . . This is the saga of one of the greatest submarine cruises of all time, the fifth and last war patrol of a fighting ship—the U.S.S. *Tang*—ably conducted by her courageous commander and his crew of daring officers and men . . .

Although Subpac gave top priority to the sinking of Japanese shipping, its SS, too, as we said earlier, were used for special missions, though none as foolish as the foe's I-boats so often had to undertake. For example, during fast carrier operations "lifeguard" submarines were stationed close to the carriers' target to rescue pilots whose planes went down at sea. When B29's began bombing Japan from the Marianas, their crews too had the comfort of knowing that SS were strung out beneath their flight path to pick them up, should they have to ditch. All told, in this way more than 600 pilots and aircrewmen were saved.

SS also transported secret agents to enemy-held islands to put them ashore under cover of darkness in inflated rubber life rafts. Often too they carried arms, radio sets, and other supplies to guerrilla forces in the Philippines and to the network of coast watchers who ferreted out Japanese ship and troop movements in the Bismarck Barrier. And at times they themselves were, of course, the "coast watchers" who flashed the first word that an enemy fleet was under way, as they did in the Battle of the Philippine Sea.

Finally, specially rigged fleet submarines were frequently used as minelayers because they could sneak into Japan's home waters, which no surface minelayer dared approach, and plant mines on the enemy's marine doorstep. But as SS *Whale* and her skipper, Comdr. John Azer, discovered on the very first of Subpac's many mine plants in Imperial waters, laying mines along Japan's heavily patrolled and protected coastline was a task that called for steel nerves.

Whale's objective was Kii Channel, the eastern entrance to the Sea of Japan and a main highway for Japanese maritime traffic. At moonrise on 24 October 1942, *Whale* nervously felt her way into the mouth of the Channel, with her lookouts intently scanning the sea for mines and grimly aware of the irony of a minelaying SS creeping through a minefield to plant mines. After nearly brushing one Japanese contact mine, *Whale* spread her mines where Azer thought they'd do the most damage and then, again ironically, sailed out of the Cannel with the help of the enemy's own navigation lights.

At dawn, *Whale*'s periscope watch saw a convoy heading into her spread of mines just seconds before a patrol boat sighted the periscope and forced the sub under. While under, though, four explosive rumbles told *Whale*'s crew that they hadn't labored in vain. *Whale* then spent several days in the same perilous waters, moving in at times to within 500 yards of shore to take periscope pictures of military and shipping installations of value to Naval Intelligence.

Whale somehow escaped being spotted until just as she was leaving for home. Then a destroyer gave her a rough time. The first depth charges opened seams, ruptured valves, and created serious leaks in her stern compartments. With her buoyancy threatened by the water she was taking in, the submarine began to settle slowly and at the same time develop a dangerously sharp upward tilt. Nor did it help her feverishly working damage control parties when more depth charges came so close that they shattered *Whale*'s light bulbs and sent slivers of glass slicing into their faces and eyes.

As Commander Azer said later, "We barely held our own with the leaks. All spare men were sent forward in a desperate effort to regain an even keel. Charge after charge was dropped, and we were pursued for 17 hours. I suppose the Nips were a little mad because we'd invaded their home territory. But we finally shook our hunter and spent a night on the surface, repairing damage. Then we hit for home, photographs secure and minefields planted for the harvest season."

Special war patrols like those mentioned above were of course ordered by Commander Submarine Force, Pacific. (In the Atlantic, it should be said, the Royal Navy's submariners performed many of the same duties, with the same display of valor.) As the Pacific War neared its close, though, submarine activities went into the doldrums. Japanese shipping had been all but driven from the seas, and our submariners suddenly found themselves with no more worlds to conquer.

It was an intolerable situation for men who thrived on danger and action. So to relieve the boredom, SS skippers began to dream up special missions of their own, to stir up a little excitement and at the same time annoy the enemy. One skipper, for instance, went so far as to put a landing party ashore to blow up a Japanese railroad bridge. Another brazenly sailed into several small coastal ports and torpedoed their harbor installations at point-blank range. Yet another, seeing two Jap destroyers at anchor in a harbor, boldly surfaced in full view of them, hoping but failing to entice them into a fight.

Most notable though was the exploit of Comdr. Eric Barr, who led SS *Bluegill* on a one-ship amphibious operation against Pratas Island, southeast of Hong Kong, then radioed Com-Subpac:

> Captured Pratas Island. Softened up island with bombardment by *Bluegill,* sent ten-man landing force ashore, encountered slight opposition, raised American flag 29 May with appropriate ceremonies, installed plaque commemorating ourselves, destroyed Japanese meteorological station and a 2000-gallon fuel dump. Please have invasion medals struck immediately! Now on to Tokyo!

Having paid homage to Subpac, it is now time to return to the surface of the Pacific and the fiercely fought battles that followed the fall of the Marianas.

CHAPTER 11

Prelude to Sho-1

By the late summer of 1944 there were but a few island stepping-stones to Japan left to occupy. In the tiny Bonin Islands, north of Saipan and only 650 miles from Tokyo, there was Iwo Jima. But Iwo was too small to serve as a base for an invasion force of the size needed for a final assault on Japan and valuable only for its strategically located airfields. Farther to the west were Luzon, the most northern of the sprawling Philippine Islands, and Formosa and Okinawa, each an island large enough to support an invasion army. Besides, with Luzon 900 miles, Formosa 700, and Okinawa only 350 miles from Japan, the three islands were spaced like rungs in a "ladder" leading directly to the enemy's homeland.

For a time the Joint Chiefs of Staff thought of leapfrogging the Philippines and setting up invasion bases first on Formosa, then on Okinawa. However, General MacArthur strongly opposed this plan. He insisted that it would be dishonorable for the United States to ignore its promise to liberate the Philippine people at the earliest possible moment. He pointed out, too, that in the Philippines, and particularly on Luzon, strong guerrilla bands were waging daily warfare against their Japanese conquerers. Thus, he argued, Luzon would be a safer base from which to launch an invasion than Formosa, where, as conquerers, we in our turn would be harassed by guerrilla attacks from that island's hostile inhabitants.

In the end the Joint Chiefs accepted MacArthur's arguments up to a point, as the timetable they drew up for the final months of 1944 indicates. On 15 September MacArthur's South Pacific forces were scheduled to capture Morotai Island; Nimitz' Central Pacific Forces, Peleliu. Morotai would then be used as a springboard to Mindanao—the most southerly of the Philippine Islands. The occupation of Peleliu, in the Palau group, would eliminate those islands as a threat to MacArthur's eastern flank, and at the same time provide a staging-point for Philippine-bound shipping and aircraft.

In October, Nimitz was to occupy Yap and Ulithi in the Caroline Islands. Ulithi was wanted as a fleet base because its deep and sheltered lagoon was only 900 miles from the central Philippines. Yap was to be taken to deny the Japs a base from which they might otherwise mount attacks on shipping anchored at Ulithi. In November, MacArthur would begin the liberation of the Philippines with a landing on Mindanao. And on 20 December, Nimitz and MacArthur would combine forces to invade Leyte, the key island in the central Philippines. Following Leyte, though, the Joint Chiefs reserved the right to decide whether to land next on Luzon or leap to Formosa.

When the plan was drawn up each step in it seemed necessary. Yet within a week of its being put into effect a chink was discovered in the enemy's armor that enabled the Joint Chiefs not only to speed up their timetable but also cancel out two entire amphibious operations.

The chink was uncovered by our fast carriers, whose assignment from 12 to 15 September was to raid the enemy's airfields in the Philippines and beat back any planes that might threaten our Peleliu landing on the morning of the 15th. Sailing within sight of shore, our carrier pilots bombed airstrips at will and easily destroyed 200 enemy planes. More important, they discovered that Japan's then air strength in the Philippines was too weak to protect even those islands, much less menace our Peleliu operation. The news of this unexpected weakness was sent to the Joint Chiefs on the evening of the 15th, along with a recommendation that the Morotai, Peleliu, Yap, and Mindanao operations be cancelled as unnecessary, and that plans be drawn up instead for the 7th and 3d Fleets to assault Leyte two months ahead of schedule, on 20 October.

(The 3d Fleet was simply the 5th Fleet operating under a new command team. With the tempo of the war increasing, Nimitz had named Admiral Halsey, Commander 3rd Fleet and Adm. Theodore Wilkinson, Commander 3rd 'Phib Force, to spell Admirals Spruance and Turner. Thus, while one command team was at sea fighting, the other could work ashore planning the next move, and no time would be lost between operations. The fighting ships remained the same except for their designations. Mitscher's fast carrier force, for example, was designated TF 58 under Spruance, TF 38 under Halsey; Admiral Lee's battleship force either TF 54 or TF 34.)

Since Halsey had taken the fleet to sea in September, it was his recommendation that the Joint Chiefs received. And they showed their faith in the veteran admiral's judgment by cancelling the Yap and Mindanao landings, advancing the date for occupying undefended Ulithi to 23 September, and approving 20 October as the invasion date for Leyte.

But there was nothing the Joint Chiefs could do about Morotai and Peleliu, since landings had been made on both islands on the morning of the 15th, just hours before they received Halsey's dispatch. It didn't matter in the case of Morotai because that lightly defended island fell in a single day, in a virtually bloodless battle. At Peleliu though the Marines met 5,300 Japanese as strongly entrenched and as determined to fight to the last man as their counterparts at Betio. And although they were eventually wiped out, they took 1,950 Marines with them—a particularly tragic loss because Peleliu didn't fall until 24 November, and by then the Battle for Leyte Gulf had already become a naval

LCI's unload troops on the beach at Morotai, September 1944.

legend and Peleliu had lost its strategic importance.

Once the new date for the Leyte offensive was approved, Halsey sailed off to soften up the enemy and at the same time keep him guessing. Between 21 September and 14 October the 3d Fleet raided Luzon, sent a cruiser force far to the east to bombard Marcus Island, moved closer to the enemy's homeland than any U.S. surface force had dared venture since Hornet's morale-boosting raid on Tokyo in 1942 to strike at Okinawa, then turned south and spent three days lambasting Formosa.

Over Luzon, Mitscher's pilots got only 18 planes; poor pickings compared to the 200 they'd destroyed in their 12/15 September foray. The shelling of Marcus—a feint to trick the enemy into thinking we were preparing to invade the island—failed because Japan's warlords had already guessed that our next target would be one of the rungs in the Philippines-Formosa-Okinawa ladder and laid their plans accordingly. But at Okinawa and Formosa TF 38 drew unexpected blood, for on those islands it found many of the planes the enemy was hoarding like a miser, to use when he knew for certain which rung in the ladder he would have to defend.

In a dawn-to-dusk raid on Okinawa, Mitscher's pilots bagged 111 planes, and in addition so flattened the island's ground installations that Okinawa was temporarily eliminated as a staging base to the Philippines. Our losses were 21 planes, six of whose pilots were picked up by a lifeguard SS.

But it was the three-day raid on Formosa that really hurt the Japanese. Fearing that the prolonged attack was the preliminary to an amphibious assault, the Japs put about a thousand of their hoarded planes into the air, with catastrophic results. For in one of the war's fiercest air battles they lost 550 aircraft and hundreds of pilots while also suffering major damage to Formosa's airstrips and other ground installations—a fearful price to pay for downing only 79 American planes and damaging two U.S. cruisers and a carrier.

A Marine Corsair cuts loose with eight 5-inch rockets over Okinawa.

In sum then, when the 3d Fleet turned south on 15 October to join our Leyte invasion force, already at sea, it had in a month's time sharply reduced the air forces the foe had assembled to counter our invasion of the Philippines. And in so doing it had robbed the Imperial Fleet of most of the air support it needed to help it carry out Sho-1, as Japan's scheme for the defense of Leyte was called.

Sho-1, which has been called "the greatest gamble, the most daring and unorthodox plan in naval history," was born of the Imperial Fleet's desperate situation following the Battle of the Philippine Sea. In that engagement, you'll recall, Ozawa lost three of the Fleet's seven carriers, more than 400 planes, and almost as many pilots. These losses broke the back of Japan's naval aviation beyond repair, because it was impossible for the Japanese, though try they did, to train replacement pilots for their four remaining carriers in time to use them in the fight for Leyte. Consequently, their still powerful surface fleet of 64 warships was naked to air attack except for what protection could be given it by land-based planes.

To further complicate matters, American submariners were sinking tankers so fast that there was a serious fuel shortage in Japan. As a result, Adm. Soemu Toyoda, Commander Combined Fleet, didn't dare keep his battleships and cruisers in home waters but instead had to base them close to their fuel sources at Lingga anchorage near Singapore. Yet his carriers were tied to the home islands by their futile pilot-training program. So it was this handicap—a supposedly combined fleet which was widely separated—plus the geography of the Philippines that largely shaped the outlines of Sho-1.

As a glance at the map will show you, two main straits lead from the South China Sea to Leyte Gulf: San Bernardino Strait north of Samar Island, and Surigao Strait running between Mindanao and Leyte. In executing Sho-1 the warships at Lingga were to steam north toward these straits, with a stop at Brunei Bay, Borneo, to refuel. There the force would divide. The Center Group of 5 battleships, 12 cruisers, and 11 destroyers would steam through San Bernardino Strait at night, led by Adm. Takeo Kurita aboard his flagship, the cruiser *Atago*. The Southern Group of two battleships, four cruisers, and eight destroyers, under Adm. Shoji Nishimura, aboard battleship *Yamashiro,* would approach Leyte Gulf by way of Surigao Strait. The two forces would then come together at dawn like the jaws of a pair of pliers, and crush all of the thin-shelled American amphibious shipping trapped in the Gulf.

The most cunning phase of the plot, though, was the role given Ozawa's Northern Force of four carriers, two old battleships, three cruisers, and eight destroyers. Ozawa was to be a sacrificial decoy. He was to come down from Japan and lure the 3d Fleet north and away from the mouth of San Bernardino Strait, so that Kurita could sweep down on our invasion shipping unchallenged. By deliberately moving within range of Halsey's air searches, Ozawa would be inviting total destruction. But if his destruction earned Kurita a safe passage through the Strait the price would not be too high, since carriers without pilots have little value.

This then was Sho-1; a daring plan, based on stealth and deception, which committed to action all that remained of the Imperial Fleet—including four carriers with a mere 116 planes on their flight decks!

Our combatant forces consisted of Kinkaid's 7th and Halsey's 3d Fleets. Halsey had 17 carriers, 6 battleships, 17 cruisers, and 64 destroyers. To provide shore bombardment and close air support for MacArthur's 145,000 troops, the 7th Fleet had 6 old battleships—5 rescued from the mud of Pearl Harbor—18 escort carriers, 8 cruisers, and scores of destroyers, destroyer escorts, and PT boats. And between them the two fleets' carriers could muster approximately 2,000 planes.

So much for the background, plot, and participants in what was far and away the most remarkable sea fight of the war.

CHAPTER 12

✲✲✲✲✲✲✲✲✲✲✲✲✲

Hornets vs. Elephants

The battle was triggered by the U.S. minesweepers that entered Leyte Gulf on 17 October to sweep safe channels to the beachheads. They were of course spotted and reported to Admiral Toyoda, as well as Gen. Tomoyuki Yamashita, commanding the 300,000 men of the 14th Imperial Army based on Luzon. Toyoda ordered Sho-1 to get under way at once, and Yamashita immediately began to assemble 45,000 troops to reinforce the single division holding Leyte.

On 18 October, Rear Adm. Jesse Oldendorf steamed through the mineswept channels with the 7th Fleet's fire support ships to commence bombarding the landing beaches, and two days later the 3d 'Phib Force began what was perhaps the easiest landing of the war. There was no surf, no mines, no underwater obstacles. And aside from some mortar fire there was little immediate enemy reaction, the Japanese garrison having chosen to retire to prepared positions in the high hills inland to await reinforcements before making its stand. As a result, by midnight 22 October the amphibious phase of the operation was all but completed, for by then we had landed 132,000 men, 200,000 tons of supplies, and secured a beachhead that included two small airstrips.

The crucial naval phase of the operation began only hours later. First blood was drawn by two submarines, *Darter* and *Dace,* that intercepted Kurita's Center Force in the approaches

189

After disembarking from LST's, these veterans of amphibious invasions stack sandbags for gun emplacements on beach at Leyte.

to San Bernardino Strait at dawn on 23 October. After sending off a contact report—the first news we had of what the enemy was up to—*Darter* put two lethal torpedoes into *Atago*, forcing Kurita to shift his flag to the superbattleship *Yamato*. (*Yamato* and her sister ship *Musashi* were the largest battleships ever built; almost half again as big as the biggest U.S. battlewagons, with 18-inch guns that fired shells 50 percent heavier than the shells of our 16-inchers.) *Darter* then disabled *Takao* while *Dace* was blowing up *Maya*. But Kurita, though shaken by the loss of three cruisers, steamed on.

In response to the SS contact report, Halsey ordered the 3d Fleet to converge on San Bernardino Strait. Shortly thereafter he got a second contact report from *Enterprise* search planes that had spotted Nishimura's Southern Force heading toward Surigao Strait. However, since Kurita's reported strength was considerably greater than Nishimura's, Halsey decided to take on the Center Force and leave the Southern Force to Oldendorf's battleships and cruisers inside Leyte Gulf.

When the 3d Fleet reached the mouth of San Bernardino on the morning of the 24th it was greeted by the enemy's only major air attack of the day, some 180 land-based planes. Most of them were either shot down or turned back. But one dive-bomber hit *Princeton* with a 500-pounder that ploughed into the light-carrier's torpedo stowage compartment, setting off an explosion so tremendous that it not only finished the carrier but also made a wreck of cruiser *Bermingham* alongside her. Then it was TF 38's turn.

For the next six hours deckload after deckload of Mitscher's planes dove down on the Center Force, their pilots' eyes widening as they saw for the first time the world's two largest naval targets, *Yamato* and *Musashi*. For six hours, too, strike after strike returned with glowing reports of cruisers "in flames," *Kongo*-class battleships "down at the bow," and innumerable claims of torpedo and bomb hits that had left *Musashi* "dead in the water"

The USS Princeton *in flames after the crew had abandoned ship and our own torpedoes administered the "coup de grace."*

A Japanese Zuiho-*class carrier maneuvers to escape further blows after having been hit by torpedoes and bombs from Navy planes.*

and *Yamato* "crippled and trailing oil." Finally, at 3:30 in the afternoon the sixth strike of the day brought back word that Kurita had reversed course and was "in full retreat westward at 22 knots."

Like all experienced commanders, Halsey knew that pilots' combat reports cannot be trusted. They are always overly optimistic because fliers *want* to believe they've scored hits. And they're usually inaccurate because a pilot diving through clouds, battle smoke, and thick AA fire is often unable to judge with certainty what type warship he is attacking. Yet for some unexplained reason Halsey chose on this of all days to believe his pilots' exaggerated claims that they had shattered Kurita's fleet.

Consequently, when a search plane located Ozawa's carriers northeast of Luzon at 4:40 that afternoon—where they'd been circling impatiently for hours, waiting to be discovered—Halsey took the bait. Just as the planners of Sho-1 had hoped, he ordered the entire 3d Fleet 300 miles north to "intercept" Ozawa's decoy force—without leaving so much as a picket destroyer to cover San Bernardino Strait.

In justice, this was Admiral Halsey's only mistake in an otherwise heroic war record. It's true, too, that he had no way of knowing that Ozawa's carriers were all but helpless because they were so short of planes. But it's equally true that the powerful 3d Fleet could have continued to block the Strait and handled Ozawa, too, had Halsey divided his force. In fact, a division of forces was so obviously called for that when the 7th Fleet's admirals received Halsey's clumsily worded announcement that he was going north, they took it for granted that he had done the obvious, and dismissed Kurita from their minds.

They thought from the dispatch's confused wording that Halsey had gone north only with TF 38, and that he had left Admiral Lee's battleship division, TF 34, behind to cover the Strait. But as Halsey said later, he'd seen no reason not to take his entire fleet with him because he'd assumed that Kurita really was retreating with a fleet "that had been so heavily damaged that it could no longer be considered a menace to the 7th Fleet." Unfortunately, it was a false assumption that came perilously close to costing us the day.

For while Kurita had reversed course, retreat had never entered his mind. His only thought was "to retire temporarily from the zone of enemy air attacks and resume my advance when . . . [circumstances] permitted." Moreover, he had a far healthier fleet with which to resume his advance than our pilots had reported. He'd suffered a major loss when *Musashi* sank after taking 19 torpedo and 17 bomb hits, and he'd had a cruiser put out of action. But he still had *Yamato* and three other battleships, eight cruisers and all of his destroyers. Thus at sunset, when the 3d Fleet's move north "permitted" Kurita to turn east again, he was still a serious menace to the 7th Fleet, and he still hoped to rendezvous with Nishimura in Leyte Gulf as planned.

There would be no rendezvous though, because Nishimura's Southern Force was steaming into an ambush. Admiral Oldendorf had lined the 35 miles of Surigao Strait with 26 destroyers and 39 torpedo boats, all poised to strike at the enemy's flank. And knowing the narrowness of the Strait would force the foe to push through it in column formation, one ship behind another, he had deployed his six battleships and eight cruisers in a horizontal line across the Strait's thin mouth. It was a classic example of "crossing the T"—a textbook maneuver wherein a commander works his ships into a position that allows them to fire their full broadsides against an opposing fleet that can only fire its forward-pointing guns.

Although the Southern Force of two battleships, four cruisers, and eight destroyers nosed into the ambush just after midnight of the 24th, Oldendorf held his fire until the enemy column was deep into the narrow waters. Then he struck at both of Nishimura's flanks with his PT's and destroyers, and from dead ahead with his heavy guns. It was no contest. As an observer said, "Oldendorf not only crossed the T, he dotted thousands of Japanese eyes."

Caught in a crossfire of torpedoes and hurtling shells, Nishimura was killed and both of his battleships and three of his destroyers were sunk in short order. The rest of his ships turned tail, but only two cruisers and five destroyers escaped the holocaust. Left behind were two cruisers and a destroyer so badly battered that they were crippled ducks for the planes that found and sank them at dawn.

In no other engagement of the war did the U.S. Navy come as near to making a clean sweep as it did at Surigao, or at so small a cost—one PT boat lost, one destroyer damaged. But, then, in no other battle except the one Halsey was waging with Ozawa that same morning did the Navy enjoy such overwhelming power.

And since Halsey's strength was so superior to Ozawa's there is as little to tell about their clash as about the one-sided encounter between Oldendorf and Nishimura. In brief, the 3d Fleet sank Ozawa's four carriers—including the sole surviving Pearl Harbor veteran, *Zuikaku*—and three destroyers and a cruiser as well.

Thus Halsey easily achieved his goal; the destruction of all that remained of Japan's carrier fleet. But Ozawa had succeeded in his mission too. With his sacrificial bait he had lured Halsey away from San Bernardino Strait. And this cleared the way, as one writer said, for "Kurita's hawks to swoop down on the 7th Fleet's chickens."—And what followed was by all odds the most remarkable sea battle of the war.

The chickens that met Kurita's hawks head on were the 18 escort carriers of the 7th Fleet. And escort carriers (CVE's in naval shorthand but "Combustible, Vulnerable and Expendable" to their crews) were never meant to fight a battle line such as Kurita's. Built on merchantship hulls, they had no armor-plating and were so thin-skinned that their sailors jokingly warned visitors "to walk lightly and don't drop anything on deck heavier than a cigarette butt."

Moreover, CVE's were neither armed nor trained for surface slugging. Aside from their AA batteries they had only a single 5-inch "peashooter." As for training, the handling of jeep carriers in a surface clash wasn't even mentioned in the Navy's tactical manuals, much less practiced. Nor were CVE air groups taught to attack warships. Their training was in antisubmarine warfare, flying combat air patrols, supporting amphibious operations, and attacking pillboxes and other shore installations. And the bomb-lockers of CVE's were stocked almost exclusively for such missions. At Leyte, for instance, on average each CVE carried

100 depth charges and 400 general purpose bombs (none heavier than 500 pounds) which while effective against shore targets were fairly feeble missiles to throw at heavy armor plate.

As a "just in case" precaution, though, each CVE did carry six aerial torpedoes and 24 semiarmor-piercing 500-pound bombs. So in their David-and-Goliath clash, the baby flattops had at least a few sharp stones for their slingshots when they went against Kurita's giants. And they also had a weapon of immeasurable worth—a band of young pilots willing to fly their hearts and if necessary their lives out.

At first light on 25 October the CVE's were as usual divided into three task units of six carriers each, with the code names Taffy 1, Taffy 2, and Taffy 3. Each unit, in turn, was screened by seven or eight destroyers and destroyer escorts, nicknamed "Small Boys." As usual, too, Taffy 1 was stationed off the southern tip of Samar Island (see map), Taffy 2 some 30 miles to the north, and farther north and nearest to San Bernardino Strait was Adm. Clifton Sprague's Taffy 3, destined to bear the brunt of Kurita's guns.

In the predawn murk of the 25th, too, all three Taffies launched planes; some for routine antisubmarine and combat air patrols, some in support of the troops on Leyte, others to chase down the enemy ships fleeing Surigao Strait. Consequently, about half of the 253 fighters and 143 bombers the CVE's could still put in the air were miles away to the southwest when the bad news came out of the north after sun-up. (A CVE normally carried 30 planes, as against a fleet carrier's 90, but the Taffies had lost so many planes during the previous seven days' operations that they could muster only 387 on the 25th.)

First to discover that TF 34 had not corked the neck of San Bernardino Strait was Ens. William Brooks of Taffy 3's antisubmarine patrol, who at 6:45 radioed Admiral Sprague, "Enemy force of 4 battleships, 8 cruisers, 11 destroyers sighted 20 miles northwest you, closing at 30 knots." Message away,

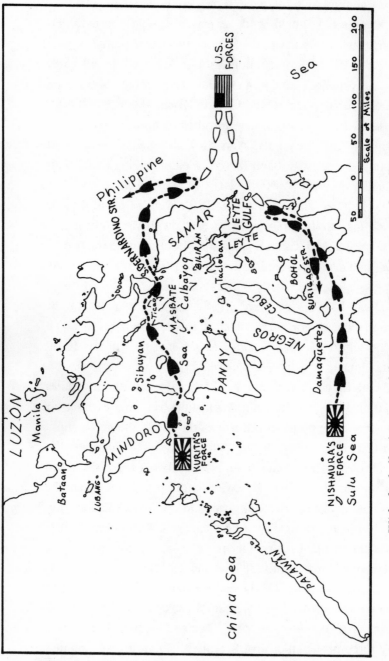

With the bulk of our naval forces pursuing a decoy north of Luzon, Japanese cruisers and battleships attempted a pincers movement against the landings in Leyte Gulf. To everyone's astonishment, they were beaten off by a "lightweight" force of American destroyers, torpedo boats and escort carriers in one of the strangest naval battles

Brooks then dove alone through the flak of Kurita's whole fleet and dropped his antisubmarine loading—two measly depth charges—on a heavy cruiser! It was a display of raw courage that would be repeated a hundred times before the morning ended.

At first, Sprague couldn't believe his ears. But as he said later, he became a believer in short order:

> It was only minutes before we made visual contact and the Jap big battlewagons opened up with their heavy stuff at 18 miles . . . At the time I didn't think we'd last 15 minutes, what with 22 warships bearing down on us at twice our top speed. But I decided we might as well give them everything we had before going down. So I ordered all carriers to launch strikes, and called back on the double all planes that were over the beach on support missions. At the same time I ordered all ships to lay smoke screens. Then I asked Rear Adm. Felix Stump of Taffy 2 and Thomas Sprague (no relation of mine) of Taffy 1 for air support, and Admiral Kinkaid for surface help.

But Kinkaid couldn't send help. The 7th Fleet's heavies were so short of shells after seven days of shore bombardments and the engagement with Nishimura that they were even then seeking out ammunition ships. And no matter how quickly they were replenished, they would then still have to steam for three hours to reach Taffy 3's position. There was no way Kinkaid could fatten his skinny force of CVE's in time to save them from what seemed certain destruction.

Left out on a limb alone, the CVE's had to fight for their lives with what few weapons they had. What followed, understandably, was not a typical naval battle that can be described neatly, maneuver by maneuver, but rather a wild free-for-all. To add to its confusion, Kurita made the mistake of ordering "General attack"—meaning every ship for itself—instead of forming an orderly Battle Line with his big ships and committing his light ones to carefully calculated torpedo attacks. Consequently

the engagement developed into a helter-skelter brawl in which
so many things took place at the same time, both on the sea and
in the air, that to make sense of the battle it's necessary to separate the surface encounters from the aerial action, even though
they overlapped in time.

The moment salvos began falling inside his formation, Admiral
Sprague turned Taffy 3 southwest, away from the Japanese. But
with the CVE's top speed being only 18 knots, within 30 minutes
Kurita had closed to about eight miles and brought his big guns
into short range. Of the surface action that followed, Sprague said
later:

> At this point (7:16 in the morning) some urgent counteraction
> was demanded, and this was the time for my little group of
> Small Boys to charge our big tormentors. In they went, pressing
> their torpedo attacks to close range most heroically, and without
> a single one being lost! Results were obscured in the heavy
> smoke screen, but we know that one destroyer got a hit on a
> battleship, another a hit on a heavy cruiser. More important,
> the Small Boys turned the enemy aside momentarily and created
> a diversion of immense value.
>
> As the Japs came within our range, I ordered the carriers to
> open fire with their peashooters (the single 5-incher each car-
> ried). As he watched the one on the *St. Lo* plug away, an old
> gunner's mate was heard to mutter, "We oughta fire that thing
> under water. We could use a little jet propulsion right now."
>
> At any rate, *St. Lo,* singling out a light cruiser astern and closing,
> scored three hits and started a large fire. *Kalinin Bay* got three
> hits too, one on a destroyer and two on a cruiser. And as *White
> Plains'* little 5-incher banged away, one of her battery officers
> sang out, "Just hold on a little longer, boys. We're sucking them
> into 40-mm. range."
>
> Now two heavy cruisers were abeam of us to port, where they
> began delivering salvos from as close as five miles. On the star-
> board side a group of cruisers and destroyers had closed range
> to five miles too. In the rear the battleships kept at an eight-mile

range. The Japs were now firing on us from three sides, and straddles and hits were being scored all over our formation.

Within this three-sided "box," my carriers were in a circle, with the destroyers and destroyer escorts in a larger circle around them. I kept my formation on a southwesterly course, but zigzagged from one side to the other, depending on which side was throwing the hottest fire. Inside our circular formation, the individual carrier skippers maneuvered violently, heading for salvo splashes on the assumption that the next salvo would land somewhere else, as the Jap gun-spotters corrected their sights. This was our pattern for most of the 2½ hours we were shelled. During this time I figure they fired about 300 salvos, letting go at two-second intervals.

Between 8 and 9 o'clock . . . my flagship, *Fanshaw Bay,* was hit six times. *Kalinin Bay* suffered 16 hits that created a shambles below decks, and only the heroic efforts of her crew kept her going. Damage control parties wrestled under five feet of water to plug up big holes in the hull. Engineers worked knee-deep in oil, choking in the stench of burned rubber. Quartermasters steered the ship from the emergency wheel aft, as fires scorched the deck they stood on. And all hands risked their lives to save mates in flooded or burning compartments.

At 8:20 *Gambier Bay* was hit so heavily that she lost the use of one engine. Her speed reduced to 14 knots, she fell back into the Jap fleet. As the big enemy warships heaved abeam at 2000 yards, they pumped 20 8-inch shells into her unarmored hull until she sank . . . Later, rescue craft out of Leyte Gulf picked up about 700 of her 900-man crew.

The Jap cruisers kept on firing broadsides at us from five miles and I never did figure out why they didn't close to two or three miles and polish us off. Around 8:40, though, their fire from the starboard was punishing us so unmercifully that something had to be done. So I ordered the Small Boys to get between us and the cruisers to throw up a heavier smoke screen and do what they could to fend off the enemy with their peashooters and any torpedoes they had left.

They gave everything they had in a desperate, valiant effort to

The damaged USS Gambier Bay *on the horizon is bracketed by shells from the Japanese fleet during the second battle of the Philippine Sea.*

protect the carriers. But in charging the Japs they ran head-on into the raking fire of some of the enemy's heaviest guns, and destroyers *Hoel* and *Johnston* and destroyer escort *Roberts* went down, their peashooters firing to the end. The Japs knew gallantry when they saw it too, I learned later, because one survivor saw a Japanese cruiser skipper salute as *Johnston* took her last plunge . . .

To me it was a miracle that under such terrific fire for that length of time only one carrier had been sunk. Two others had been badly hurt, but three were untouched. Still, it seemed only a matter of time until Taffy 3 was wiped out. And since a couple of battleships and cruisers had slipped past us and begun dumping shells inside Taffy 2's formation, things didn't look good for Admiral Stump either.

Then at 9:20, after giving us all they had in the way of surface fire, which was pretty poor, the Japs sent in their destroyers for a torpedo attack, launching 14 fish on our starboard quarter. And again they showed their timidity by striking from too far away—about five miles—so that when the torpedoes reached us they were near the end of their rope and, fortunately, almost parallel to our course. So it had to be about 9:25, because I was still concentrating on dodging torpedoes, that I heard someone on the bridge yell, "Damn it, they're running away!"

I couldn't believe my eyes, but it did look as if the whole Jap fleet was retiring. Then our planes overhead reported that Kurita had indeed changed course. And still I couldn't get the fact into my battle-numbed brain. At best, I'd expected to be swimming by this time . . .

But Kurita was not running away. He had changed course because he wanted to assess his battle damage; to regroup his fleet, which as a result of his unwise "General attack" order had become too widely scattered to maneuver as a unit; and to gain time to study the tactical situation, which he found puzzling. Then, if it seemed wise, he intended to resume course to Leyte, this time with his fleet in an orderly antiaircraft formation. And behind all of his reasons for breaking off action at that time lay one thing—the ferocious air attacks he was undergoing. They had hurt him, they had helped scatter his fleet, and they puzzled him.

The attacks were coming largely from the carriers of Taffies 3 and 2. (Taffy 1, farthest south, threw a few planes into the fray at first, then became so busy fighting off land-based Jap planes, in an encounter to be described later, that it could no longer help.) And after the war one of Kurita's staff officers said, "Even in comparison with the many experiences we'd had with your fleet carriers, this was the most skillful work of your planes we had seen." This was high praise for a small band of fliers untrained in attacking warships, and a surprising compliment too. For not until the climax of the fighting were the CVE's able to send off a full-fledged "strike" in the strict military sense of the word. During most of the action, in fact, they were lucky if they could group as many as a dozen planes together for an assault.

Taken by surprise, in danger of swift annihilation, and with unarmed planes left on their flight decks after the routine morning missions had flown off, the CVE's simply couldn't afford to indulge in the time-consuming luxury of massing their aircraft for carefully coordinated strikes. Instead, they had to arm and launch planes with desperate haste, singly or in small groups, with orders not to concentrate on any one enemy ship but to cripple and stop as many as possible as quickly as possible. As a result, one observer said, the hurriedly launched pilots had to go after Kurita's fleet "like a swarm of angry hornets attacking a herd of elephants."

The first swarm of hornets to reach the herd was one of the morning's largest. Flown off by Taffy 3's *Kitkum Bay* about 7:30, it consisted of 6 bomb-carrying TBF's and 12 fighters, led by TBF pilot, Comdr. Richard Fowler. Weaving through the blinding flak of the Jap fleet, Fowler scored a direct hit amidship on battleship *Nagato* while his companion TBF's were holing heavy cruiser *Suzuya* so badly that she began to flood and slowly sink. Forced into the shelter of a cloud bank by the heavy AA, Fowler then tried to regroup his unit, but in the murk of the clouds he and three other TBF's got separated from the rest of the flight. Yet even though they now had no fighters to run interference for them, the four planes then plummeted down on heavy cruiser *Chikuma*, planted nine 500-pounders on her deck, and had the satisfaction of seeing her blow up and sink in five minutes. (Later, Fowler's wingman said, "The Commander flew in so low he could spit down *Chikuma*'s funnel, then laid his last bomb smackdab on her bow. Man, I'm glad he's on our side!")

While Fowler was drawing first blood, another comparatively large flight of Taffy 3 planes joined the fray; 6 TBF's and 20 fighters that had been orbiting over the Leyte beachhead when Kurita was sighted. The bomb-shackles on the fighters' wings were loaded with small rockets and the Navy TBFs bomb-bays mostly with 100-pound bombs, for use against shore targets. Yet as one of the flight pilots said, "We may have had nothing but creampuffs to throw, but we worked some of those Jap ships over so thoroughly that I bet their topside personnel had a pretty sticky time of it for a while."

For the most part, though, Taffy 3's planes attacked either singly or in groups of two or three, in a piecemeal fashion that led to innumerable feats of individual heroism. Time after time lone TBF's made runs on Kurita's ships without benefit of fighter cover to strafe and clear the decks ahead of them of AA gunners. Then, as often as not, the lumbering torpedo-planes would turn and themselves strafe their targets until their ammunition was exhausted. In one instance, a TBF pilot whose guns were as empty as his bomb-bay braved AA fire for an hour, making dry runs on cruisers in a courageous effort to throw off their firing for a few precious minutes.

In another case, a TBF pilot, who by mistake was catapulted into the air without a bomb load, first made repeated dummy torpedo runs on the enemy's heavies in the hope of turning them aside, then switched to making strafing runs on *Nagato* to divert its AA gunners while another lone TBF was planting its torpedo in the battleship's bow. And in yet another instance, a flight leader saw one of his men about to challenge *Yamato*'s 120 AA guns with all two of his TBF's forward-firing machine guns. Yelling into his mike, the flight leader ordered the young flier to break off his suicidal run and return to his carrier for more bombs. Back came the suspiciously meek reply, "Aye, aye, sir. But, damn it, he started shooting at me first."

Fighter pilots were given a free hand to strafe, in hopes they would kill enemy gunners, silence their weapons, or, more important, divert attention from the CVE's. When they found an armed TBF they would of course run interference for it too. Then when they exhausted their ammunition, almost to a man they followed Lt. Paul Garrison's example. After his F6F's guns went silent he spent another hour in the air searching out bombers who still had missiles to drop. He found 10, then made 10 dry strafing runs on Jap warships, twisting and turning above them in a deliberate attempt to lure their gunners into firing at him rather than the attacking TBF's.

While Taffy 3's hornets were swarming, Admiral Stump's Taffy 2 carriers armed and launched 43 TBF's with torpedoes and 36 F6F's with 500-pound semiarmor-piercing bombs slung under each wing, in the record time of 1½ hours. (In their reckless haste to get planes airborne, Taffy 2's flight-deck crews sometimes used sledgehammers to pound fused bombs and torpedoes into their release-shackles more quickly!) As might be expected, the pilots of these planes matched Taffy 3's in guts and gumption. To cite just one example, taken from the log of Stump's flagship, *Natoma Bay:*

At 8:45 Lieutenant (JG) Leon Connor made a bombing run through heavy flak on a battleship but did not drop because the ship turned too sharply. Connor then made a second run on a cruiser and claims a hit. Clearing the flak, Lt. Connor discovered a TBF circling behind a cloud. The unknown pilot called him on radio, saying he had a torpedo and asking Connor to go in ahead of him and strafe. Connor agreed. Pitting his two machine-guns against the AA batteries of the Japs for the third time, Connor led the unknown pilot with his precious torpedo in a two-plane attack on cruiser *Chokai,* braving heavy flak. Connor looked back when he cleared the hail of AA fire and saw the torpedo go home in the cruiser's belly. But the other plane had been hit and was falling. It flamed for a few seconds on the sea, then disappeared. No one got out.

As it happened, no one got out of 43 of the 105 planes lost to Jap antiaircraft fire that morning. But the death of the un-known pilot mentioned above was swiftly avenged by other Taffy 2 torpedo-planes that put the finishing touches to *Chokai,* sinking her just minutes before Kurita ordered his fleet to re-group.

Thus when Kurita broke off the action he had taken worse than he'd given. He had bagged one jeep carrier, two destroyers, and a destroyer escort. But he was short four heavy cruisers. *Chokai* and *Chikuma* had been sunk; slowly sinking *Suzuya's* decks were awash; and leaking *Kumano,* her speed cut to 15 knots by a torpedo from one of Sprague's destroyers, was limping toward the safety of San Bernardino Strait. Even so, he still had 4 powerful battleships, 4 cruisers, and 11 destroyers; all capable of 24 knots, none so badly damaged its fighting ability was lessened to any great degree. So if he had acted promptly he could easily have brushed past the CVE's into Leyte Gulf. And once there, Oldendorf's battle line, still feverishly loading ammunition, would have had trouble stopping Kurita from zeroing in his heavy guns on a beachhead black with our men and supplies, and on our thin-skinned huddle of supply ships in the Gulf.

But instead Kurita kept his ships milling around aimlessly for two hours, not setting course for Leyte again until 11:47. After the war, he said that during those two hours he was not only assembling his ships and checking their battle damage, but also trying to collect a vital piece of information concerning his tactical situation. For although he had learned by radio that Nishimura had been turned back with heavy losses, he hadn't heard a word from Ozawa up north. Nor could any radio station he questioned give him any information about the outcome of Ozawa's mission. (It was learned later that Ozawa's messages telling Tokyo and Kurita that he had succeeded in luring the 3d Fleet out of position were sent via a faulty radio transmitter that didn't transmit!)

So not knowing where Halsey's force was, Kurita was fearful that the 3d Fleet might be lurking nearby. And to support his fears, some of his staff officers, who were unable to see clearly through the heavy smoke screen thrown up by Taffy 3, had identified Sprague's CVE's as *Independence*-class light carriers, and his *Fletcher*-class destroyers as *Baltimore*-class cruisers (their silhouettes were much alike)—both of them types of ships found only in the 3d Fleet. In addition, Kurita had intercepted the plain language calls for help Kinkaid had sent to Halsey, and he couldn't imagine that Kinkaid would be asking for help that was beyond reach.

Thus it was Kurita's overactive imagination, not what he knew, that made it difficult for him to make up his mind as he circled with his fleet. As Admiral Nimitz said after reading Kurita's postwar statement, "The radio intercepts in particular left him with the impression that 3d Fleet carrier forces might be converging on him from all directions. Though the horizon was empty, he felt surrounded . . . [felt] Leyte Gulf might be a trap."

In the end, Kurita conquered his fears and decided to make one last attempt to break through to the Gulf. But his indecision had cost him the day, because when he turned his guns away from the CVE's he handed them an opportunity he had denied them while he kept them under fire. He gave Admiral Stump two untroubled hours in which to assemble, arm, and launch 72 planes. Some of them were Taffy 3 planes that had had to land on Stump's carriers because their own flight decks had been holed by Jap shells; the rest, Taffy 2's planes. Between them the 35 TBF's and 37 fighters formed the largest launch of the day. More important, it was not only the first fully coordinated strike the CVE's had had time to get into the air but the first of their strikes that had all of the earmarks of one launched from a fast carrier group.

The strike was led by Commander Fowler, whose deeds during his eight hours aloft that day earned him the distinction of being the "most valuable single aviator in the battle." After his low-level drops on *Nagato* and *Chikuma,* Fowler had landed on Taffy 2's *Manila Bay* in a TBF riddled with 30 bullet holes. Then he had called Stump and said, "I'll be loaded and ready to take off at 11:20. How many planes can you give me? Give me any kind of a strike and we'll turn the s.o.b.'s."

When Fowler rendezvoused with the planes Stump "gave" him, his first order was, "We'll attack no cripples, no destroyers. We're going after the healthy, heavy bastards." Then he headed for Kurita's fleet and, after circling it and studying the cloud cover, sent half his force behind one cloud bank and led his own section behind another. Next he formed his planes into small groups and assigned each group a specific target. That done, he asked, "Everybody set?" When all answers were affirmative he said, "Okay, let's go." Nosing over at full throttle, 72 planes then hurtled down on the enemy force in unison. Fowler got two hits and a near miss on a *Kongo*-class battleship. His wingman clobbered heavy cruiser *Tone*'s after turrets. And at least six other Jap heavies were either hit or jolted by damaging near misses.

For Kurita the strike was the last straw. Its size and skillful execution convinced him that what he imagined was true. Now he was sure that he was within range of the 3d Fleet, and that his only hope of surviving to fight another day lay in flight. So he ordered a hasty retreat, and confessed his defeat in a message to Tokyo: "Have abandoned penetration of Leyte Anchorage . . . proceeding north . . . [will] pass through San Bernardino Strait."

The rest is anticlimax.

While Kurita raced north, Taffy 2 recovered planes and put together another strike. But since his CVE's had expended all of their torpedoes and semiarmor-piercing 500-pounders, Stump was forced to load the day's last strike with bombs too small to be lethal. Even so, when the Center Force reentered San Bernardino Strait at 9:40 on the night of the 25th, only one of its ships—a destroyer—had escaped damage.

As for the 3rd Fleet, it didn't reach the Strait until just after midnight, for while Halsey had eventually broken off his pursuit of Ozawa in response to Kinkaid's calls for help, he had done so too late to intercept Kurita. On the morning of the 26th, though, TF 38 got off three strikes, totaling 257 planes, that managed to sink light cruiser *Noshiro* and further damage already badly battered *Kumano*.

So when Kurita reached Brunei Bay, Borneo, on 28 October he still had a fleet of sorts; 4 battleships, 6 cruisers, and 10 destroyers. Yet for the Japanese it was small consolation because Sho-1, the all-out gamble, had been a total failure.

The statistics tell part of the story of the enemy's crushing defeat in the far-flung three-day four-part Battle for Leyte Gulf. Of the 216 U.S. ships engaged only seven were lost; one light carrier, two CVE's, two destroyers, one destroyer escort, and a PT boat. Of the 64 Japanese warships involved, 28 were sunk—4 carriers, 3 battleships, 10 cruisers, and 11 destroyers— and most of the others were at least partially crippled. Thus at Leyte, for all practical purposes the Imperial Navy ceased to exist as an effective fighting fleet, and Japan's days as a major sea power were ended.

But there was more to the encounter than cold statistics. As naval historian Samuel Eliot Morison says, "The Battle for Leyte Gulf did not end the war but it was decisive. And it should be an imperishable part of our national memory. The night action in Surigao Strait is an inspiring example of . . . faultless execution. And the CVE's battle off Samar was the most gallant naval action in our history, and the most bloody—1,130 killed, 913 wounded. The story of that action, with its . . . [Small Boys] making individual attacks on battleships and heavy cruisers; its naval aviators making dry runs on enemy ships to divert gunfire from their own; and the defiant humor and indomitable courage of bluejackets caught in the ultimate of desperate circumstances, will make the fight of the 'Taffies' with Kurita's Center Forces forever memorable, forever glorious."

Yet even as we were dealing the Imperial Navy a blow so devastating that it would never again dare engage in a major action, the Japanese in turn were embarking on an ominous new form of warfare. For it was at Leyte that the Kamikaze Corps made its first appearance. And in the war's final months the suicidal tactics of this dread Corps would take a heavier toll of U.S. ships and men than the Imperial Navy's now-silenced guns had accounted for in three years of combat.

CHAPTER 13

The "Divine Typhoon"

In the Sho-1 plan, Adm. Takijiro Ohnishi's Philippines-based First Air Fleet was assigned the task of repelling U.S. warships. But Halsey's repeated raids on the Philippines prior to Leyte had, as Ohnishi said, "destroyed nearly two-thirds of my aircraft." So on 19 October he told his men, "With so few planes we can succeed only by suicide attacks. Each plane must be armed with a bomb and crash-landed on a warship's deck." Then he called for volunteers and his pilots, raised in the Shinto religious belief that to die for the emperor is "a bridge to heaven," offered themselves almost to a man.

By Ohnishi's orders, his volunteers were not to fly in formation but singly, and do everything possible to sneak past American combat air patrols in what amounted to a deadly game of hide-and-seek in the skies. They were to attack in one of three ways. They could come in low on the water, "wave-hopping" to avoid being picked up by the sky-searching radar screens atop the masts of U.S. warships; they could dive unexpectedly out of a low cloud formation; or they could make their dives with the blinding rays of the sun at their back. Anything to avoid being exposed to AA fire for more than a few seconds as they bore in on their targets.

Ohnishi sent his first suicide mission out on the morning of the 25th. It was a small flight of six planes led by Lt. Yukio Seki, and its victim was Taffy 1. (This was the raid, mentioned in the last chapter, that kept Taffy 1 from sending all-out aid to Taffy 3.) Seki's Zekes went into almost vertical dives at 10,000 feet, each aiming for one of Taffy 1's six CVE's. Three were shot down. The fourth exploded in the water so close to *Sangamon* that it tore small holes in the carrier's hull. Though peppered by flak, the fifth and sixth, respectively, crashed *Santee* and *Suwannee*. Fortunately, neither carrier suffered heavy losses, both put their fires out in short order, and emergency repairs enabled them both to resume flight operations before nightfall.

The day's second suicide mission struck at Taffy 3, two hours later, just as Sprague's carriers were beginning to think their ordeal was over. It was a flight of eight planes. One hit *Kitkum Bay* a glancing blow and bounced into the sea. Four were splashed. Two, even though aflame from AA hits, struck *Kalinin Bay* staggering but not fatal blows. And one burst through *St. Lo*'s flight deck, set off the bombs and torpedoes on her hangar deck, and sank her with heavy losses.

This was the small but destructive beginning of what Ohnishi called the "body-ramming" tactics of the Kamikaze, or "Divine Typhoon," Corps, so named for a typhoon that broke up a Chinese invasion fleet that sailed against Japan in the Middle Ages. And once the tactics Ohnishi had developed became known to the Imperial Army Air Force it too formed a Kamikaze Corps, because it was clear that body-ramming solved many of the problems handicapping the enemy's air power.

A kamikaze plane on a one-way trip had twice the range of a bomber flying a round trip. It could be flown by an overage or a half-trained pilot as readily as by a veteran aviator. Using planes as guided missiles enabled the enemy to throw into the fray hundreds of obsolete aircraft, including training planes and even ancient biplanes. Last but far from least, Ohnishi's two small raids had proved that by flying singly and using hide-and-seek tactics some planes could always sneak past our combat air patrols. And once a suicide plane was within range of its target there was no sure defense against it except a highly unlikely direct 5-inch hit. Not that many wouldn't fall victim to AA fire. But because of the momentum they built up in their dives, many others could be trusted to plunge on into American ships even though they had had wings shot off or been set aflame or had their pilots killed by 40-mm. or 20-mm. fire.

With good reason then, when the enemy began staging planes to Luzon to support General Yamashita's 14th Imperial Army, about two-thirds of their pilots wore the insignia of the Kamikaze Corps—a cherry blossom with three petals, symbolizing the fleeting nature of life. And, ironically, although the enemy's original air weakness in the Philippines had enabled the Joint Chiefs of Staff to speed up their timetable for invading Leyte, the situation was now reversed. For the added strength given Japan's air arm by the kamikazes now played as large a part in forcing the Joint Chiefs to delay their timetable for the liberation of the Philippines as did the enemy's unexpectedly stiff and prolonged defense of Leyte.

Following Leyte, the JCS had scheduled an amphibious assault on Lingayen Bay, Luzon, for 20 December, to free Luzon. After that, Iwo Jima was to be invaded on 20 January 1945, Okinawa on 1 March. But largely due to the fanaticism of the wearers of the cherry blossom insignia, none of these dates was met.

The ground fighting for Leyte had a lot in common with the struggle for Guadalcanal, both because it was slowed down by heavy rains and because the inland waterways between Luzon and Leyte had a slot down which Yamashita could send his version of the Tokyo Express to reinforce Leyte. Yamashita lacked the cruisers and destroyers that had covered the original Express, of course, but he did have plenty of kamikazes. And it was their vicious attacks on the destroyers the Navy sent in to halt the flow of reinforcements that allowed Yamashita to land 45,000 troops on Leyte's west coast during the first month of

Navy gunners firing 40-mm guns at kamikazes.

A close-up of a kamikaze plane just before it crashed into the USS Essex.

This photograph, taken from the USS Ticonderoga, *shows kamikaze crashing on the flight deck of the USS* Essex.

the campaign, and thus retain a grip on the island for weeks longer than we had anticipated.

Nor was that all the kamikazes accomplished. In the same month they also scored heavily on TF 38, which had taken over the air support of the Leyte operation from the CVE's. On 30 October, *Intrepid, Franklin,* and *Belleau Wood* were body rammed and forced to retire briefly to Ulithi for repairs. On 5 November a kamikaze killed 50 and wounded 132 of *Lexington*'s crew, without doing much hurt to the ship. And on the 25th, *Essex* and *Cabot* took a kamikaze apiece, while ill-fated *Intrepid,* just back from Ulithi, was taking two more that cost her a 100 men and earned her the nickname "The Evil I."

Thus in four weeks' time an infant Kamikaze Corps not only forced the Joint Chiefs to alter their timetable but also schedule an additional amphibious operation. For it was now clear that before landing on Luzon—where the enemy's chief strength lay and where he had dozens of airfields—we needed an island base from which Army fighters could take off to give added

Kamikaze attack on the USS Intrepid.

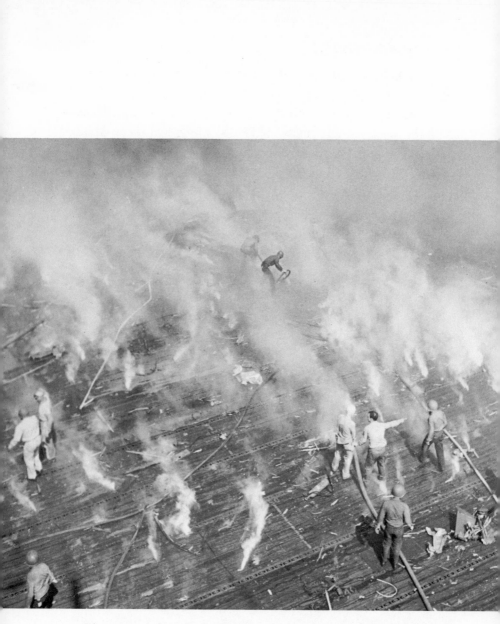

The crew of the USS Intrepid *battle fires following a kamikaze crash.*

protection against kamikazes to our Lingayen convoys and landings. So the Lingayen operation was postponed from 20 December to 9 January 1945, and in its place an amphibious assault was launched on 15 December against Mindoro, an island close to Luzon and known to be lightly defended.

In the Mindoro operation, the kamikazes again took their toll. They sank three LST's, crippled a destroyer, and rammed cruiser *Nashville* so brutally that she limped back to Leyte with 323 dead and wounded. Still, Mindoro was taken so quickly that by Christmas, Army P-38's were able to use it as a base. And but for their help the passage of our Luzon Attack Force from Leyte Gulf to Lingayen Gulf, 100 miles north of Manila, might have been even bloodier, and it was bloody enough as it was.

The Luzon Attack Force included most of the 7th Fleet's ships that had taken part in the invasion of Leyte and, with the exception of a few battalions left behind to mop up the now cornered Japs on Leyte, the troops of the 6th Army. Rendezvousing on New Year's Day, 1945, Admiral Oldendorf's 164 warships sortied three days in advance of the transports and supply ships, to allow for a 3-day interval of shore bombardment at Lingayen. Passing through Surigao Strait into the Sulu Sea, in the first three days of the voyage our CVE planes and P-38's splashed most of the 100-odd kamikazes sent against the bombardment force, and those that got through missed their marks. Then the force's luck ran out.

On the 4th, a twin-engined bomber dropped out of the sky like a meteor, somehow unseen by any radar in the fleet, and sank CVE *Ommaney Bay,* with a loss of 100 lives. The following day, cruisers *Louisville* and *Australia,* CVE *Manila Bay,* DE *Stafford,* and LCI-70 were hard hit, but survived. Then on the 6th the force entered U-shaped Lingayen Bay—and there for three nightmarish days the Navy experienced for the first time the nerve-shattering savagery of an all-out kamikaze attack.

Navy cruiser anti-aircraft gun crews strain to identify the nationality of a plane overhead.

In a frantic effort to cling to Luzon, the enemy had assigned every flyable plane in the Philippines to a suicide mission, except for a handful reserved to fly high ranking officers to Formosa if need be. The planes were cleverly camouflaged on more than 60 airfields—too many to be neutralized even by the combined efforts of TF 38, the Army bombers now flying from Leyte, and the Mindoran P-38's. And to make matters worse, the hills rimming Lingayen Gulf all but blacked out the 7th Fleet's radars.

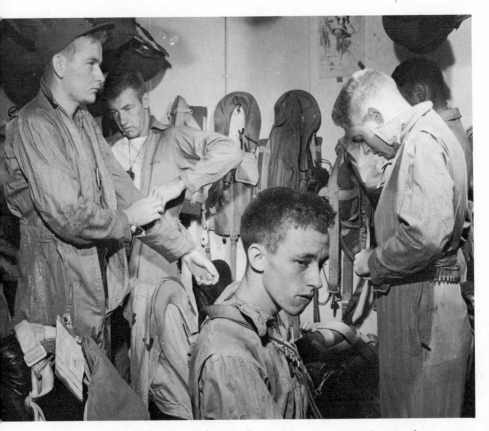

Air crewmen grimly put on their flight gear in preparation for another strike.

The box score tells the grim story. In three days, 27 ships were crashed, 10 of them seriously. They included two battleships, four heavy cruisers, three CVE's, nine destroyers, a seaplane tender, three landing ships loaded with tanks, and four minesweepers, three of which were sunk. It was the worst mauling the Navy had known since 1942, when it had reeled before the enemy's superior strength in the seas around Guadalcanal. Even so, throughout the ordeal every ship held its station and continued to pour its salvos on the landing beaches.

This was true even of unlucky *Australia,* which was rammed three times. After taking her third kamikaze, her skipper reported that he had 39 dead and 56 wounded, and that less than a third of his AA batteries could now fire. Then he added calmly, "We are continuing the bombardment"—and drew from Oldendorf the admiring reply, "That's the stuff winning navies are made of!"

By the night of the 8th, though, the Japs had expended most of their planes, since countless more had been shot down or had crashed into the sea than had hit their zigzagging targets. On the 8th, too, all of the senior naval officers on Luzon flew off to Formosa, knowing that there was now no way of halting our landing and that the future defense of Luzon was now in the hands of Yamashita's 300,000-man army.

The landings began on the 9th, and by the 13th our troops were all ashore and moving off the beachhead. The story of the arduous seven-month campaign for Luzon that followed belongs of course to the Army. It should be said, though, that military experts agree that Yamashita's stiff resistance was strategically senseless, for reasons summed up by Admiral Ralph Ofstie:

In January 1945 Japan was in fact a defeated nation. . . [because] the Philippines were lost then. But more important was what was lost with them. The chief prize for which the war was fought, the so-called Southern Resources Area with its reserves of oil, was gone and blockading American fleets could sail freely to the shores of eastern Asia. Japan's hopes of future resistance depended upon oil, and now the oil was completely cut off. Her surface fleet was gone, and so were thousands of aircraft expended in defense of her supply line. Suicide tactics were now Japan's last hope, and even these economical defense methods suffered from the blockade. Gasoline was so scarce that pilot training had to be cut to a bare 100 hours, and in the Inland Sea the Imperial Navy's few surviving ships could barely muster enough fuel oil to get under way. . . Japan was defeated: It remained only necessary to persuade her of the fact.

The terrible and tragically pointless task of persuasion began in February, at Iwo Jima.

Since October 1944 our Marianas-based B29's had been bombing Japan and, to quote a Japanese source, they were beginning "to rock the nation to its very foundations." But they were also suffering prohibitive losses in planes and crew members, and one of the chief reasons was Iwo Jima. Lying 650 miles south of Tokyo, this tiny volcanic island served the enemy well. Its radars gave Tokyo two hours' warning of the approach of our B29's, which was more than enough time to alert AA crews and get interceptor planes airborne. Fighters from Iwo's two airstrips were in a position to pick off wounded B29's lurching home from Tokyo. And Japanese medium bombers could take off from Iwo to raid our air bases on Saipan and Tinian.

If we had a strong need to rob the Japanese of Iwo, we had advantages to gain too. Iwo would give us a base from which our long-range P51 Mustang fighters could escort B29's to Tokyo and back. Crippled B29's could land at Iwo for emergency repairs. And with Iwo as a refueling station our medium-range bombers could carry explosive payloads to Japan too.

The job of taking Iwo was given to the Marines and to Admiral Spruance's command team, which meant that the 3d Fleet became the 5th Fleet once again. D-day was 19 February, but the pre-invasion pounding of the island was begun 2½ months earlier. It was carried out in part by land-based bombers that dropped 6,800 tons of explosives on the small island during that period, in part by surface ships which plastered Iwo with 22,000 rounds of 5- to 16-inch shells. This was the most intensive softening-up treatment given any Pacific island to date. Yet it made scarcely a dent in Iwa's prepared positions, because the barren eight-square-mile island was a fortress unlike anything we'd ever before encountered. Betio's defenses had seemed rugged, but compared to Iwo's they were crude.

Uninhabited except for its 20,000-man garrison, Iwo was a

concrete honeycomb of connected strong points. Mixing the island's volcanic ash with cement, the Japanese had emplaced hundreds of artillery pieces, mortars, and antitank guns in bunkers whose walls were four feet thick and reinforced with armor plate. More than 800 pillboxes encircled the island's two airstrips, not to mention the hundreds that lined its shores. Entire hills had been hollowed out and rebuilt on the inside with networks of caves, some 40 feet deep, that sheltered both men and heavy guns. The island's many natural caves—some big enough to hold 400 men—had been reinforced too, and even wired for electricity.

So although the island looked as pockmarked and bleak as the moon when the 5th Fleet reached it on 16 February, its bomb craters meant little. Iwo's deeply dug in defenders were ready and waiting. Nor were they much disturbed by the three days of additional bombardment the 5th Fleet laid on them. Consequently, when the Leathernecks hit the powdery volcanic sand of the invasion beaches on the 19th, they walked into what their commanding general, Holland Smith, called "the most savage and the most costly battle in the 168-year-history of the Marine Corps."

It took the Marines 26 days to secure the small island, as against four at Betio, because Iwo literally had to be taken foot-by-foot by men crawling forward on their stomachs behind tanks that not infrequently bogged down in the volcanic ash. Since the enemy neither asked for nor gave any quarter, hundreds of innocent-looking mounds of earth, that turned out to be concrete pillboxes and blockhouses, had to be taken with rifles, grenades, flame-throwers, or bayonets. Most of the enemy's innumerable underground positions had to be taken with the same hand weapons, in eye-to-eye fighting. There were times too when the Marines, their grenades gone and their rifle clips exhausted, finished cleaning out caves with their only remaining weapon—their sheath knives.

Admiral Nimitz said of Iwo that it was the battle "where

The amphibious assault by Marines on Iwo Jima, 19 February 1945.

uncommon valor was a common virtue." Yet it was anything but a spectacular encounter, with valiant charges and counter-charges. Rather it was an exhausting and grisly struggle with a strongly entrenched enemy that fought almost to the last man (of the 20,000-man garrison only 216 surrendered). And to win the bitter struggle the Marines had to send in the largest force they'd ever committed to a single battle, 60,000 men. Of this force more than 20,000 were killed or wounded. So Iwo, sadly, was also the costliest battle in Marine history.

During the operation the 5th Fleet's support ships stood close inshore, duelling with the enemy's coastal guns, providing rolling barrages, keeping the nights bright with star shells, doing every-thing possible to help the embattled Marines. At the same time, our carrier planes were over Iwo every daylight hour, their pilots often spending nine hours in the air in a single day, strafing, bombing, or making pinpoint rocket attacks on the few enemy positions their missiles could reach.

For the first few days air opposition was almost nonexistent; partly because of Iwo's distance from Japanese air bases and partly because TF 58 had raided Japan on the 16th and 17th and destroyed an estimated 500 planes in the Tokyo area. Then, late in the afternoon of the 21st, came the Flash Red signal, followed by the "Man all battle stations!" call over the fleet's loudspeakers. Radar had picked up a 50-plane flight coming in from the north.

As it turned out, half were torpedo-planes, half kamikazes. None of the torpedo-planes was successful, but in the approaching darkness the kamikazes did better. True, one merely skidded across CVE *Lunga Point*'s flight deck, leaving a roaring if not serious gasoline fire in its wake. *Saratoga,* though, was holed by four suicide planes that tore up her decks, set her afire, and caused 315 casualties. But the tough old veteran was not to be downed. Her damage control parties got her fires under control and her wounds patched in a matter of hours, and *Saratoga* then

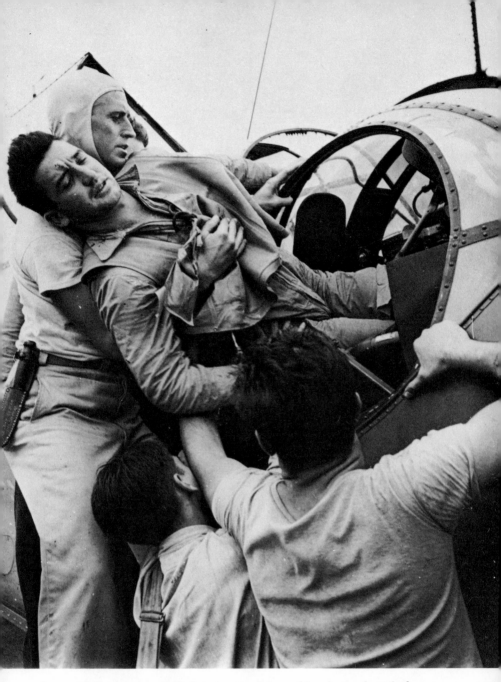

A wounded aircrewman being removed from his plane aboard the carrier USS Saratoga.

A kamikaze crosses flight deck of USS Lunga Point, *leaving roaring gasoline fire in its wake.*

steamed back to a west coast repair yard under her own power.

CVE *Bismarck Sea* was less fortunate. As the sun set she was hit aft by a kamikaze that detonated her store of torpedoes and turned her into a flaming torch. Destroyers were ordered to stand by the stricken vessel. At 7 in the evening the "Abandon Ship" order was given and 900 men plunged into the heaving ocean, their small life jacket flashlights blinking on and off as the high waves hid them from view. At 9:15 the *Bismarck Sea,* now a mass of flaming white-hot metal, turned over and sank. The rescue destroyers put out their small boats and searched all through the night, but 218 of the carrier's crew drowned in the darkness and rough water.

Considering the combined losses of the Marines and the Navy (6,802 killed) the price paid for Iwo Jima's eight square miles of land was high indeed. Yet the capture of Iwo almost certainly saved more lives than it cost. By the war's end more than 3,000 B29's had made emergency landings on the island, and the bulk of them, with their ten-man crews, would probably have been lost without the haven of Iwo. As one B29 pilot said, "When I had to land on Iwo Jima, believe me, I thanked God and the men who had fought and died for it."

CHAPTER 14

✦✦✦✦✦✦✦✦✦✦✦✦✦✦

The Fleet That Came To Stay

With Iwo Jima secured all eyes turned to Okinawa—the last and greatest stepping-stone on the long and winding road from Pearl Harbor to Japan. Sixty-seven miles long by up to 20 wide, the hilly island was a land of forests, steep limestone ridges, and deep ravines that lent themselves to the enemy's genius for constructing a defense-in-depth. Besides its strong garrison, Okinawa was also inhabited by a half million hostile civilians. And the island lay within easy flying range of the 55 airfields on Kyushu, the southernmost of the home islands.

Being as determined to hold an island only 350 miles from their homeland as we were to take it, the Japanese had devised a series of defensive strategies that were all built around one word—"suicide." On Okinawa itself, the holding operation was entrusted to Gen. Mitsuru Ushijima's 120,000-man garrison of veterans, each of whom was asked to fight not just to the death, but to trade his life for the lives of 10 Americans, or one American tank. At sea, the plot was to send out mighty *Yamato*, with a cruiser and eight destroyers, to fight to the last and take what American warships they could with them when they sank—and to make sure the suicide squadron carried out its mission faithfully it was given only enough fuel for a one-way trip and food for only five days.

In the air, the Imperial High Command planned to use the Kyushu-based 6th Army Air Force and the 5th Air Fleet. Some of their aircraft would be employed in conventional bombing and torpedo attacks, some in small kamikaze raids. But at least 2,000 planes were assigned to Operation Ten-Go: a plan calling for 10 massive and coordinated kamikaze attacks which, hopefully, would so wreck our fleet that it could never again support an invasion force.

For our part, the Okinawa landings, set for 1 April, were again a 5th Fleet operation, under Admiral Spruance. But knowing that the enemy would go all-out to defend the island, this time we used more of everything than ever before—40 carriers, 18 battleships, 200 destroyers, dozens of cruisers, and hundreds of supply ships, transports, minesweepers, landing craft, salvage ships, and repair vessels. In sum, an awesome armada of 1,317 ships, with the 5th 'Phib Force's transports jammed to the gunwales with the 172,000 combat and 115,000 support troops of the 10th Army (five infantry and three Marine divisions).

And again, too, we used all the amphibious techniques we had perfected in more than three years of practice, weeks of preliminary air strikes against Okinawa's ground installations, days of heavy shore bombardment, mine sweeping, UDT's, etc. But there was one technique that we hadn't perfected—a defense against body-ramming. So knowing that at Okinawa the kamikaze menace would surely reach a ferocious peak, when D-day dawned Spruance had his fleet disposed in a new way.

As usual, TF 58 was poised offshore to counter enemy attacks and the fire support ships were close inshore, shelling the beachhead and keeping a protective eye on the huddle of cargo vessels and transports, and the landing craft ferrying ashore the first waves of troops, artillery and tanks. What was unusual was the radar picket line ringing the island in a great circle some 50 miles out from its beaches. At each picket station was a destroyer or destroyer escort with a fighter-director officer aboard who,

Amtracks move in for landing on Okinawa while battleship fires salvos at island, 1 April 1945.

when an enemy flight appeared on his radar screen, was responsible for guiding out to intercept it one of the many Combat Air Patrols being maintained constantly by 17 CVE's. By this means, hopefully, most kamikazes could be splashed before they reached our main fleet units. As for those that got through, at least our amphibious forces would be forewarned of their approach.

However, D-day at Okinawa turned out to be a true April Fools' Day. The expected heavy kamikaze attacks failed to materialize, as did the anticipated stiff resistance at the beachhead. In fact, five hours after going ashore our troops took one of the island's airfields without firing a shot. The unloading on the beaches went unopposed throughout the day too, with the result that by evening 50,000 men were ashore, along with all necessary supplies and heavy equipment. Equally surprising, the unexpected quiet continued for nearly a week, leading one puzzled infantryman to say, "I don't get it. I've already lived longer than I thought I would."

The reason things seemed to be going too easily was that Ushijima, a shrewd general, had pulled most of his garrison back to the southern quarter of the island. He knew that if he met us on the beaches much of his forces would be chewed up by our naval guns and air power. And he hoped by concentrating his troops behind carefully prepared defense lines in the south to lure our ground forces into a position where they could not be supported by naval gunfire, and then wipe them out.

Consequently, the 10th Army met little resistance as it spent its first days ashore cleaning out the northern part of the island. But when it turned south it promptly ran into a string of pillboxes of such strength that they even had steel doors which defied flame-throwers. These were merely the outposts of Ushijima's "iron rings," his defense-in-depth Shuri Line, and they made it plain that, just as at Iwo, our troops were once again going to have to slog their way forward yard by yard.

For the 5th Fleet, the first five days were unnaturally quiet too. Only a few kamikazes appeared, only a destroyer and five transports were crashed, and only one, a transport, was left a useless hulk. It was nothing like what had been expected, and sailors were beginning to mutter that Okinawa was "the screwiest damn place in the Pacific."

Then on the evening of 6 April, word came from two of our SS patrolling off the coast of Japan that *Yamato,* cruiser *Yahagi,* and eight destroyers had sortied. Their move was timed to coincide with the first Ten-Go attack, and the squadron was supposed to bring its heavy guns to bear on any U.S. ships the kamikazes damaged but failed to sink. Stupidly, though, the Japanese left their suicide squadron naked of air cover. So when Spruance told Mitscher, "You take 'em," he did it without much trouble.

During the morning of the 7th, Mitscher maneuvered into a position to launch, and at noon the first of his strikes bore in on the forlorn enemy. In minutes a destroyer was sunk, *Yahagi* was stopped dead in the water, and *Yamato* was shaken by two bombs and a torpedo. Other strikes then piled in to sink *Yahagi* and three more destroyers, and forced the remaining four to turn tail and run. As for *Yamato,* she was holed below the waterline by so many torpedoes that she developed a sharp list and began to capsize slowly.

The final moments of the last pride of the Imperial Fleet were described by one of her few survivors, Ensign Yoshida:

> I heard the report, "Correction of list hopeless." . . . . Men were jumbled together on the deck in disorder. . . . Admiral Ito struggled to his feet. His chief of staff then rose and saluted. They regarded each other solemnly. The deck was nearly vertical and *Yamato*'s battle flag was almost touching the waves. . . . Shells of the big guns skidded across the deck of the ammunition room, crashing against the bulkhead and kindling a series of explosions. Then the ship slid under, accompanied by the blast

The battleship Yamato *blows up just before sinking after having taken eight bomb and eight torpedo hits by Navy pilots, 17 April 1945.*

and shock of compartments bursting from air pressure and the
rumble of exploding magazines.

Yamato lost 2,488, her sister ships 1,167 men. Our losses to
antiaircraft fire were only 10 planes, eight pilots and eight aircrewmen. Which helps explain why no more battleships have
been built or are likely to be. For air and guided missile power
have almost certainly brought to a close the long day of the
big-gunned ship and ended five centuries of traditional blue-water
naval warfare.

However, our losses to the first Ten-Go attack were of a far
different order. In the daylong raid on the 6th, the enemy sent
out 355 kamikazes, 341 bombers and torpedo-planes. They came
in from all points of the compass and from all altitudes; some
wave-hopping, some slanting out of low clouds, some screaming
down from thousands of feet up.

With so many planes and ships involved, thousands of words
could be written about any one of the great Ten-Go raids. But
some idea of their terrifying ferocity comes through in Admiral
Morison's brief description of what just two of our destroyers
went through during the first raid:

> Around three o'clock in the afternoon, 40 to 50 planes stacked
> at various altitudes between 500 and 20,000 feet, began orbiting
> and attacking *Bush* (Commander R. E. Westholm) . . .
> *Bush* shot down two Vals [dive-bombers] and drove off two
> more. Thirteen minutes later a Jill [a torpedo-bomber] was
> sighted heading low for her. The plane jinked and wove at an
> altitude of 10 to 35 feet above the water; and although every
> gun on the destroyer was firing, it kept coming and crashed
> between the two stacks. The bomb exploded in the forward
> engine room, killing every man there and in the two fire rooms.
> Flooding started immediately and *Bush* took a 10-degree list
> . . . the wounded were treated on the fantail or in the ward-
> room, and although the ship had gone dead, everyone expected
> to save her.
> *Colhoun* (Commander G. R. Wilson) learned by radio that

Bush needed help and began to close at 35 knots. . . . At 4:35 she reached *Bush,* apparently foundering. She signalled a support craft, LCS-64, to rescue *Bush's* crew, then tried to position herself between the sinking ship and a flight of about 15 Japanese planes. They approached, and when one went for *Bush* Commander Westholm ordered about 150 of his men fighting fires topside to jump overboard for self-protection. and trailed knotted lines for them to climb aboard again.

Colhoun fired every gun she had at an approaching Zeke, which splashed midway between the two ships. Another was hit by a 5-inch shell at 4000 yards, and caught fire. *Colhoun's* guns were then quickly trained on a third diving at her starboard bow, and the first salvo hit him square on the nose; he splashed 50 yards abeam. Just then Commander Wilson received a report that a fourth Zeke was about to crash his port bow. Too late he ordered full left rudder. The plane hit *Colhoun's* main deck, killing the gun crews of two 40-mm mounts. Its bomb exploded in the after fire room, killing everyone there. . . .

Colhoun was getting fires under control when the fifth attack within 11 minutes came in. Two kamikazes were splashed but a third crashed, blowing a great hole below the waterline and breaking the ship's keel. While the damage control parties were working, a sixth attack came in. Two planes were splashed but a third and forth crashed *Bush,* killing all of the wounded in the wardroom and starting a fierce fire. Still, neither skipper would give up his ship. At six o'clock another kamikaze crashed *Colhoun,* already so badly damaged that this additional misfortune did not make things much worse.

It was now dark. At 6:30 a big swell rocked *Bush,* whose structure was now so weak that she jackknifed and slid to the bottom. Commander Wilson of *Colhoun* now decided to abandon ship. At 7:00 destroyer *Cassin. Young* closed to take off survivors, and then sank *Colhoun* by gunfire. LCS-64 and a fleet tug did their best to rescue *Bush's* swimmers, but complete darkness had set in, a high sea had made up, and very many were drowned. *Bush* lost 94 of 307 men aboard. *Colhoun,* owing to *Cassin Young's* prompt rescue work, lost only 35.

Also sunk by kamikazes that day were destroyer *Emmons,* an LST, and two ammunition ships. Seventeen other ships were crashed—10 so badly they had to be scrapped, 7 badly enough to be out of action for a month or more. Total casualties on the 23 kamikazed ships were 466 killed and 568 wounded. And although the enemy's losses were heavy too—355 kamikazes and an uncounted number of his 341 conventional bombers—it was clear that if he could continue punishing us at this rate Operation Ten-Go might well succeed.

The "Divine Typhoon" raged again six days later when 185 kamikazes came in; "considerably damaging" *Enterprise,* crashing but only partially disabling four destroyers and battleship *Tennessee,* and body-ramming destroyer *Abele* so violently that she sank in five minutes, with heavy losses. But the 12th was in addition the day the men of the fleet learned of President Roosevelt's death. It was a loss that stunned and saddened them because the President had won their hearts both as a peerless war leader and a stout champion of the Navy, and many wept unashamedly. But under Harry Truman, the new President, there was of course no letup in our war effort—or the enemy's.

The 16th was another bad day, with 165 kamikazes concentrating on the fleet while 150 bombers worked over our troop positions ashore. *Intrepid* furthered her reputation as "The Evil I" by taking the fourth kamikaze of her career. Destroyer *Pringle* was sunk, and four others managed to survive severe maulings, though how *Laffey* remained afloat is a mystery. In 80 minutes, in 22 separate attacks, she was hit by six kamikazes and four bombs and was near-missed by a bomb and a seventh kamikaze as well. Yet even though she was a shambles topside and belching flame and smoke from every vent, *Laffey's* gallant gun crews stuck to their posts and splashed eight more suiciders before a tug towed her out of danger. Then, having survived the most intensive kamikaze assault, experienced by any ship in the war, she patched her wounds and headed for a repair base under her own power!

At this point in Operation Ten-Go, Spruance radioed Admiral Nimitz, "The skill and effectiveness of enemy suicide air attacks and the rate of loss and damage to ships are such that every

Impact and explosion of a kamikaze on the flight deck of the USS Intrepid.

means should be employed to prevent further attacks. Recommend attacking Kyushu and Formosa airfields with all available planes, including the [Marianas-based] 20th Army Air Force."

The attacks were made, but the enemy's camouflaged suicide planes were spread too thin on too many fields for the raids to be effective. So the Ten-Go onslaughts continued, and the number of damaged ships limping back across the Pacific to west coast repair yards grew. But since the 5th Fleet, to quote Admiral Spruance, "had come to Okinawa to stay the distance," the transpacific traffic was two-way. While the crippled and wounded steamed home, replacements of flesh and steel sped westward, some destroyer divisions even being ordered out of the Atlantic to join the battered 5th Fleet.

The need for replacements grew with the fourth and fifth Ten-Go raids. In the fourth, spread over 27/28 April, an ammunition ship was sunk, a transport and two destroyers were bludgeoned out of shape, and the brightly lighted hospital ship *Comfort* was crashed, killing or wounding 10 of its nurses and 78 of its patients and crew. In the fifth, on 2/3 May, in addition to 370 men we lost two destroyers and two large landing ships, and had a third destroyer and a CVE crashed. Almost unbelievably too, one of the destroyers sunk was rammed not only by two Zekes but two old wood-and-canvas biplanes!

Thus in the first month at Okinawa we had 40 ships either sunk or so battered that they had to be scrapped, and 18 whose battle damage kept them in a repair yard for at least 30 days. By then, too, it was obvious—both afloat and ashore—that there would be no quick victory at Okinawa. General Ushijima's Shuri Line was still intact, and to overcome his challenge we had to bring in an additional Army division and ever-increasing shiploads of supplies for our ground forces. So as guardians of our shipping, the sailors of the fleet settled down for a long trial by blood and fire. A war correspondent who was there, Hanson Baldwin of

The camera catches the trails of tracers and shells in a night pattern of anti-aircraft fire over Okinawa, 27 April 1945.

The New York Times, has given us a moving account of the
nerve-wracking nature of their ordeal:

> With the end of April the Ten-Go operations do not falter; the
> terrible battle is to drag on for almost two more months. . . .
> But during May and June Okinawa becomes less a struggle of
> ships against bombs and planes and more a test of human will
> and endurance.
>
> There are alerts unending. For more than 40 consecutive days
> there are air raids, large and small, every night and every day.
> The "bong, bong, bong." of General Quarters sounds night
> and day too. So sleep becomes a thing yearned for, dreamed
> about. Heads droop over gunsights; nerves frazzle, tempers snap;
> skippers are red-eyed and haggard. The Navy's system of
> breaking the enemy's codes has enabled us to forecast the days
> of the big Ten-Go attacks and warn crews the night before to
> be prepared. But this practice has to be stopped. The strain
> of waiting, the anticipated terror, made vivid from past experi-
> ence, sends too many men into hysteria or nervous breakdown.
>
> Only that saving American trait—a sense of humor—keeps
> some from the brink of horror. An AA gunner says, "You
> know what? Here we're getting the hell beat out of us, and I
> bet the Navy doesn't have a dime's worth of insurance on these
> ships." A destroyer crew, fed up with repeated brushes with
> death, rigs up a huge sign with a pointing arrow: "To Jap
> Pilots—This Way to TF 58's Carriers."
>
> Ashore, the bloody, slogging progress inches into the Shuri
> Line, but the Jap defenses hold, and on 22 May word comes
> that our troops are encountering the most effective artillery fire
> yet met in the Pacific. The rains deluge Okinawa in late May;
> fields become swamps, tanks get mired. Mud is king and am-
> munition and fuel are moved to the front in amphibious
> vehicles. . . .
>
> And the suiciders come again in swarms and coveys. . . .

In May the Ten-Go planes came three times. But they were
steadily being whittled down by our combat air patrols and AA
fire, and the eighth Ten-Go raid, 27/29 May, was the last to
which more than a hundred kamikazes were committed. Still,
in May they sank or sent to the scrap heap 30 of our warships

The USS Bunker Hill *after being hit by two kamikazes within 30 seconds, 11 May 1945.*

and crippled 5 others. One that was crippled was Admiral Mitscher's flagship, *Bunker Hill,* which lost almost 400 men and was so torn apart that she too had to join the line of ships retiring to west coast shipyards. But the dauntless little admiral—the only man on his flag bridge not to "hit the deck" when two Zekes plunged into his carrier and turned it into a floating torch—escaped injury and calmly transferred his flag to *Enterprise.*

The day the eighth Ten-Go raid ended was also the turning point ashore, for on the 29th the 10th Army broke through the Shuri Line, leaving 50,000 of Ushijima's men dead in its rubble, and began the final push toward the southern tip of Okinawa. The two final Ten-Go attacks, made the first and third weeks of June, were comparatively small—only 45 kamikazes in each—and damaged only eight ships. And on 21 June, the day the last of the Ten-Go wearers of the cherry blossom insignia perished, General Ushijima committed suicide, too. With his army annihilated and an advancing American patrol only 100 yards away, he knelt on a ledge overhanging the ocean and committed hara-kiri with his samurai sword, thus bringing to an end all organized resistance on Okinawa.

The defense of the island cost the Japanese more than 100,000 men, at least 1,900 kamikaze planes and pilots, and unknown hundreds of torpedo-planes and bombers. Okinawa's capture cost the Navy 34 ships sunk, 368 damaged, over 4,900 men killed, and some 4,800 wounded. The 10th Army lost 7,613 men and had 31,800 wounded. To put it another way, never before in one battle had the Navy lost so many or so much; never before in land fighting had so much American blood been shed in so short a time in so small an area; and never before in any three months of the war had the enemy suffered so hugely.

After the fall of Okinawa sealed Japan's fate, events moved swiftly. In July, the leaders of the nations that had already won victory in Europe—President Truman, England's Prime Minister Churchill, and Russia's Premier Stalin—met at Potsdam, Germany. They agreed that Japan should "be given an opportunity to surrender," and promised that the Allies would respect the sacred role of Emperor Hirohito in Japan's national life. The Potsdam Declaration was broadcast to the Japanese people in late July, then delivered in writing through formal diplomatic channels to the Japanese cabinet. But the Japanese government was still in the hands of a group of fanatical warlords, and they denounced the Allied peace offer as "presumptuous and unworthy of consideration."

We had hoped to shelve the plans for Operation Olympic— the invasion of Kyushu on 1 November—but now we had no choice. Reluctantly, we began to speed up preparations for the invasion, knowing that sobering as our losses at Okinawa had been, they would seem trivial compared to what lay ahead. For we knew that there were more than 2 million soldiers in the enemy's home islands. And from past experience we had no reason to believe that our intensive preinvasion air-and-naval pounding of their homeland would lessen their fighting spirit, or, for that matter, the morale of Japan's civilian population. At Okinawa, high school boys had fought side-by-side with Ushijima's troops. It was possible, then, that in defense of their country old men, boys, even women might willingly take up arms against us.

Our military planners feared that at a minimum Operation Olympic would cost us a half million casualties. It was taken for granted, too, that the enemy had reserved hordes of kamikazes for the expected invasion, and would be building more. So it was also taken for granted that from a third to a half of our fleet would be sunk or knocked out of action in the assault. All of which explains why the officers who worked out the details of our invasion plan later spoke of it as the most somber job they'd ever undertaken.

But as everyone now knows, by August the atom bomb— whose secret development was known to only a select few of the

The Third Fleet maneuvers off the coast of Japan, 17 August 1945.

highest Allied war leaders—was ready to be dropped, and Operation Olympic was set aside.

On 6 August, the B29 *Enola Gay* took off on its historic flight from the Marianas and dropped the first atomic bomb on Hiroshima. A second bomb was dropped on Nagasaki on 9 August, and on the 15th Japan surrendered. By mutual agreement, though, the signing of the formal surrender was scheduled for 2 September aboard the battleship *Missouri* in Tokyo Bay.

Flying the same flag that had waved over the Capitol in Washington the day Pearl Harbor was attacked, *Missouri* entered Tokyo Bay and anchored about 10 miles off the huge Yokosuka Naval Base on 29 August, to make arrangements for the sur-

The U.S. fleet in Tokyo Bay, with Fujiyama in the background, 29 August 1945.

The Japanese surrender aboard the USS Missouri, *Tokyo Bay, 2 September 1945.*

render ceremony. Shortly thereafter a Japanese admiral came out from the naval base to represent the Imperial Navy in the surrender discussions. And more than any words can say, the craft the admiral was forced to use to get to *Missouri* tells the story of how well the U.S. Navy played its role in World War II.

To reach the battleship he had to travel aboard a decrepit old navy tug. That he would have preferred to make the voyage in a more resplendent craft and one more suitable to his high rank goes without saying. But none was available to him. Except for a handful of destroyers and submarines in distant ports, the warships of the once proud and powerful Imperial Fleet were all fathoms deep or too beaten up to move. The men of our Navy had seen to that.

Bibliography

Asprey, Robert B., *Semper Fidelis: The U.S. Marines in World War Two*. New York: W. W. Norton & Company, Inc., 1967.

Baldwin, Hanson W., *The Greatest Sea-Air Battle in History*. New York: The New York Times Magazine, 26 March 1950, The New York Times Co.

Bliven, Bruce, Jr., *From Pearl Harbor to Okinawa*. New York: Random House, Inc., 1960.

————, *From Casablanca to Berlin*. New York: Random House, Inc., 1965.

Bryan, J. III, *Aircraft Carrier*. New York: Ballantine Books, Inc., 1954.

———— *Battle Stations: Your Navy in Action*. New York: Wm. H. Wise & Co., Inc., 1946.

———— *Campaigns of the Pacific War*. Washington, D.C.: Navy Analysis Division, United States Strategic Bombing Survey, 1946.

Carse, Robert, *Long Haul: The U.S. Merchant Service in World 2*. New York: W. W. Norton & Company, Inc., 1965.

Coale, Comdr. Griffith B., *North Atlantic Patrol*. New York: Farrar & Rinehart, Inc., 1942.

Collier, James B., *Battleground: The United States Army in World War 2*. New York: W. W. Norton & Company, Inc., 1965.

Commager, Henry Steele, ed., *History of the Second World War,* New York: Pocket Books, 1945.

Costello, Edmund L., *The Seabees of World War II*. New York: Random House, Inc., 1963.

Davis, Kenneth S., *Experience of War: The United States in World War Two*. New York: Doubleday & Company, Inc., 1965.

Fuchida, Mitsuo, and Okumiya, Masatake, *Midway, the Battle That Doomed Japan: The Japanese Navy's Story*. ed. by Clarke H. Kawakami and Rober Pineau. United States Naval Institute, 1955.

Gilbert, Price, Jr., *The Escort Carriers in Action*. Atlanta, Ga.: Ruralist Press, Inc., 1946.

Jensen, Oliver, *Carrier War*. New York: Pocket Books, 1945.

Johnston, Stanley, *Queen of the Flat-Tops: The U.S.S. Lexington and the Coral Sea Battle*. New York: E. P. Dutton & Co., Inc., 1942.

Karig, Walter and Kelley, Welbourn. *Battle Report: Pearl Harbor to Coral Sea*. New York: Farrar & Rinehart, Inc., 1944.

Morison, Samuel Eliot, *History of the United States Naval Operations in World War Two*. Boston: Little, Brown and Company, 1947–62 (15 vols.)

———, *The Two-Ocean War*. Boston: Little, Brown and Company, 1965.

———, *The Oxford History of the American People*. Boston: Little, Brown and Company, 1965.

Okumiya, Masatake and Horikoshi, Jiro (with Martin Caidan), *Zero*. New York: Ballantine Books, Inc., 1956.

Roscoe, Theodore, *United States Submarine Operations in World War Two*. Annapolis, Md.: United States Naval Institute, 1949.

Shirer, William L., *The Rise and Fall of the Third Reich*. New York: Simon & Schuster, Inc., 1960.

Smith, S. E., ed., *The United States Navy in World War Two*. New York: Ballantine Books, Inc., 1967.

Smith, Stan, *Pass the Ammunition*. New York: Macfadden Books, 1963.

Snyder, Louis L., ed., *Masterpieces of War Reporting*. New York: Julian Messner, 1962.

Sprague, Vice Admiral C.A.F. and Gustafson, Lt. Philip H., *The Japs Had Us on the Ropes*. New York: American Magazine, April 1945, Crowell-Collier Publishing Co.

Stafford, Edward P., *The Big E: Story of the U.S.S. Enterprise*. New York: Random House, Inc., 1962.

Tuleja, Thaddeus V., *Climax at Midway*. New York: W. W. Norton & Company, Inc., 1960.

Weller, George, *The Story of Submarines*. New York: Random House, Inc., 1962.

Woodward, C. Vann, *The Battle for Leyte Gulf*. New York: The Macmillan Company, 1947.

Young, Peter, *A Short History of World War Two, 1939–1945*. New York: Thomas Y. Crowell Company, 1966.

Index

(Italic figures indicate illustrations)

K